HOW TO FIGHT OFF A
FUNDAMENTALIST

*A Tactical Guide To Calling Out Christian
Arrogance, Ignorance, and Hypocrisy*

Edward M. Craig

ISBN: 1499180063
ISBN 13: 9781499180060
Library of Congress Control Number: 2014907297
CreateSpace Independent Publishing Platform
North Charleston, South Carolina

TABLE OF CONTENTS

ACKNOWLEDGEMENTS

I would like to thank my late father, the sweet-sounding tenor saxophonist Morgy Craig, whose unassuming greatness helped convince me that I, too, might someday do great things; his mother Frida, who would probably strangle me for writing this book if she were alive today, but gave me my first Bible and got me started paying attention to religion; my fabulous illustrator Christian Mirra, who brought my cartoon ideas to life; plus a variety of other folks too numerous to mention by name (including my big, beautiful, and slightly crazy family) for supporting me during the course of life and this project.

These days one often hears the abstract command to "justify your existence." With this book, I feel I might have finally done that. You can judge for yourself, and from whichever angle you approach the book, I hope you enjoy it, learn a thing or two, and never think of Christianity the same way again.

EMC

Let not many of you become teachers, my brethren, for you know that we who teach shall be judged with greater strictness. For we all make many mistakes, and if any one makes no mistakes in what he says he is a perfect man, able to bridle the whole body also. If we put bits into the mouths of horses that they may obey us, we guide their whole bodies. Look at the ships also; though they are so great and are driven by fierce winds, they are guided by a very small rudder wherever the will of the pilot directs. So the tongue is a small member and boasts of great things. How great a forest is set ablaze by a small fire! (James 3:1-5)

***

I do not believe that the same God who endowed us with sense, reason, and intellect has intended us to forego their use. –Galileo Galilei

Note: there are many different translations of the Christian Bible. This book for the most part uses the King James and the New Oxford Annotated Bibles.

FOREWORD

KNOWLEDGE IS POWER

What is the most annoying thing about Fundamentalist Christians? That's like asking—"What is the most annoying thing about being marooned on **Planet Mime?**" Of course it's that you can always walk away from these clowns, but *you can never get free!* Jesus kooks are everywhere—at work, on the street, in government, on TV—demanding an audience. And while they would prefer someone a bit more gullible, they will settle for *you*. So you need a strategy, my friend. Because let's be honest, while you keep wishing they would work on a disappearing act, they keep putting on that same old song and dance, and until now they were always more prepared for you than you were for them.

But that was before you picked up this book! I'm here to tell you that all along the solution has been knowing *more* about their crazy religion, not less. And once you learn a little, you will soon discover how little most of those pesky Christians know. Learn a lot, and you will quickly find yourself dominating one holy war after another.

"Maybe," I hear you saying, "but I don't have that kind of time for a subject that puts me straight to sleep." Well, that's the beauty of it! *I already did all the work!* I'm the guy who snuck into the opponent's headquarters and smuggled out their playbook. I'm the one who broke it all down to bite-size. So you wouldn't have to. The heavy lifting is done, and now you can know more after just a few hours of reading than they know after whole lifetimes of completely missing the point of stared them in the face every day.

Does this mean you will finally get them to shut up and leave you alone forever? *Of course not. Get real!* When a wind-up toy meets a wall, does it give up easily? Right. But you *will* stand a great chance of annoying them even more than they annoy you, which, in a war like this, will just have to do. For you have succeeded in battle, my friends, when you've made your voice echo in the ears of your adversaries.

So let's get started, shall we?

PART ONE

KNOW CHURCH HISTORY

Who exactly was this guy Jesus Christ? What is Christianity? What does it mean to be a Christian? You're about to find out.

Christianity is by far the most popular religion in the world. In 2013 a little more than two billion people, or close to thirty percent of all living human beings, claimed to be Christian (or their parents claimed it for them).

As you can see, the other religions in the world with really large followings are Islam (22 percent), Hinduism (13 percent), and Buddhism (6 percent). Another one out of seven people in the world (15 percent) claims not to be part of any organized religion at all. If that describes you, you obviously have plenty of company.

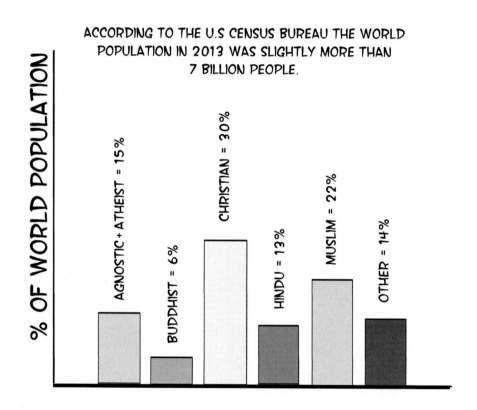

ACCORDING TO THE U.S CENSUS BUREAU THE WORLD POPULATION IN 2013 WAS SLIGHTLY MORE THAN 7 BILLION PEOPLE.

% OF WORLD POPULATION

AGNOSTIC + ATHEIST = 15%

BUDDHIST = 6%

CHRISTIAN = 30%

HINDU = 13%

MUSLIM = 22%

OTHER = 14%

These numbers are merely rough estimates of data that are constantly changing and difficult to measure accurately.

None of these groups can touch Christianity for sheer numbers, however. And with a narrow majority of its followers still loyal to the Roman Catholic Church, which prohibits birth control, none are likely to challenge it for first place any time soon.

There are many other lesser-known religions in the world, but none of them comes close to the popularity of these Big Four faiths. Christianity has held the top spot in the world at least since the European conquest and conversion of the Americas beginning five hundred years ago, and possibly for another one thousand years before that.

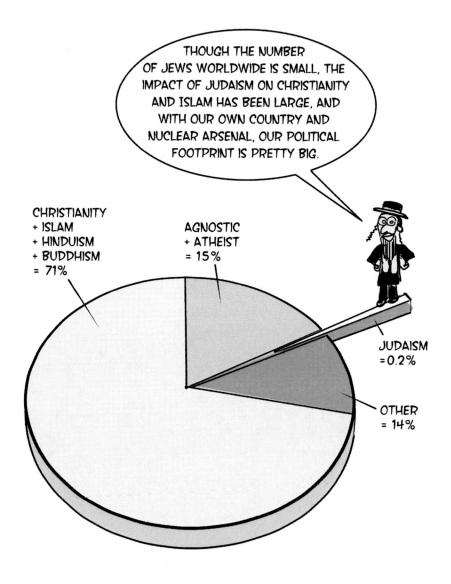

Christianity got its start two thousand years ago with the life of a real person named Jesus. You might have heard of him. Serious historians and scholars, no matter their religion (or lack of it), unanimously agree that Jesus was an actual person born to a Jewish mother in a part of the world known today as the Middle East, which sits at the eastern end of the Mediterranean Sea, right between Europe, Asia, and Africa. Not everyone agrees on the exact city or date of his birth, but *everybody* agrees that Jesus was born and lived his entire brief life as a Jew.

The main source of information Christians have for these things is a large book called The Holy Bible, which is made up of sixty-six smaller books.

The Christian Bible is the world's all-time best-selling book.

The Jews are a very old ethnic group that worships Yahweh (or, more accurately, YHWH), the god of Abraham and Moses. These iconic figures were tribal leaders and holy men that lived in the Middle East region during ancient times. By "holy men" I simply mean they dedicated their entire lives to their relationship with their god.

According to Jewish scholars, Abraham lived around four thousand years ago, while Moses, if he existed at all (it's debatable), probably came on the scene well over three thousand years ago, meaning he lived and died more than a thousand years before Jesus was born.

According to tradition, Abraham was the first Jew to make a contract with Yahweh about how a Jew should live. Strangely enough, Abraham is also a vital character in Islamic tradition. In fact many Muslims revere Abraham (or Ibrahim) as a prophet and believe the entire Arab race is descended from a circumcised Jew—Abraham's bastard first son, Ishmael. Since the story of Abraham is a crucial part of Christianity's Holy Bible that makes Abraham not just an important figure in Judaism, but also in Christianity *and Islam.*

In Jewish lore Moses helped the Jews escape from slavery under the Egyptians, received the Ten Commandments (Jewish Laws) on stone tablets directly from Yahweh on a mountaintop, then led the Jews on a meandering, forty-year search for the "Promised Land" of Canaan (now Israel). Although it is a great story, archeologists today agree that despite extensive research, no convincing evidence that the Jews were ever enslaved in Egypt has turned up—nary a word in surviving Egyptian archival records or a single shard of Hebrew pottery. *Nada.*

Given that the Jews were a group of nomadic herdsmen, however, there is every reason to believe the "meandering" part of the story.

Archeologists have fairly reliable ways up determining these things, such as sifting through ancient garbage sites for pork bones (or the absence thereof). No really, that's an actual example!

Stories about Abraham, Moses, and other Jewish historical figures are contained in what is called the Old Testament, which is the first and largest part of the Christian Holy Bible. Oddly enough, more than half of the Christian Bible is therefore made up basically of a Christian version of the Jewish Torah, and it is fair to say that nearly all of Christianity's most abusive applications of the Bible throughout history—justifying everything from countless wars to slavery to the subordination of women to the persecution of homosexuals—have been based mainly on this so-called Old Testament of the Christian Bible. I describe some of these abuses in part four of this book.

"When a man strikes his slave, male or female, with a rod and the slave dies under his hand, he shall be punished. But if the slave survives a day or two, he is not to be punished; for the slave is his money." (Exodus 21:20-21)

Technically, the Jewish Torah is just the Five Books of Moses, known as the Chumash, plus an oral tradition. But Judaism's written Bible equivalent, known as the Tanakh, is very similar to the Christian Old Testament. It contains The Books of Moses plus those books known collectively as The Prophets (Neviim) and The Writings (Kesuvim), which are also contained in Christianity's Old Testament, slightly rearranged. These include books like **Joshua, Isaiah, Jeremiah, Ezekiel, Daniel, Zechariah, Jonah,** and **Micah**. As you can plainly see, the modern baby-naming book industry is deeply indebted to these important figures from Jewish history.

Surprisingly, many of these same books of the Jewish Tanakh and Christian Old Testament are also considered "revealed scriptures" or sacred texts by members of the Muslim faith, who refer to them as the Tawrat and the Zabur. It should be noted, however, that Muslims believe the exact versions used by modern Jews and Christians have become corrupted.

Muslims even revere Jesus himself as a prophet, or enlightened being.

The Jewish Tanakh/Christian Old Testament is, frankly, filled with more violent revenge stories than you can count, and more truly perverted sex than you can fathom, considering it is supposed to be a sacred text (see in particular the books of Genesis and Exodus). Not only that, but page after page of it is devoted to bizarre behavioral rules that could not possibly be less practical or more foreign to modern Christianity (see for example the Books of Leviticus and Deuteronomy). If it is meant as a code of conduct, the Old Testament could hardly be any more widely violated by Christians today, many of whom conveniently ignore this gross hypocrisy while cherry-picking the portions of it they relish using to condemn the conduct of others.

These rules include many dietary restrictions prohibiting the consumption of, to name just a few: pork, any kind of blood (including the blood in meat), and aquatic animals without fins or scales. Also strictly forbidden are tattoos, planting more than one kind of seed in a field, clothing made of mixed fabrics, and beard-trimming or hair-shaping. Prohibited sex acts include sex during menstruation, homosexuality, and rape of a virgin. According to Deuteronomy 22:28-29, however, rape of a virgin is excused if you marry the victim, pay her father fifty shekels, and never divorce her. No, I am sadly not making this up.

In fairness, however, many parts of the Old Testament make for compelling reading, some because of their epic storytelling and others because of their poetic beauty or comforting sentiment. When modern Christians aren't using it to support fire-and-brimstone lectures full of threats of eternal damnation, they prefer to think of the Old Testament in these kinder, gentler terms. The book of Psalms, for example, contains many soothing passages that are read as a structural element of traditional Christian worship services.

Another example would be the "Song of Songs" (also known as the "Song of Solomon"), a book that is essentially a lengthy romantic love sonnet written in ancient Hebrew and thought by some to be included in the Bible as an allegory of Jesus's love for his bride, the Church. Parts of it border closely on the erotic.

* FROM *THE SONG OF SOLOMON 7:7-9*

But let's get back to our subject: the Jew named Jesus. According to the Christian Bible, Jesus was born in a Jewish town called Bethlehem, which is now part of the Jewish country we call Israel. Everyone agrees he grew up Jewish in a Jewish city called Nazareth, which is now part of the Islamic quasi-country we call Palestine. The larger Jewish area where he lived and worked and preached was (and still is) known as Galilee, which is now an agricultural region in northern Israel, populated these days by a non-Jewish, Islamic majority.

If you need help understanding just how Jewish Jesus was, repeat the word BETHLEHEM to yourself a few times. While you're doing it, think about Tevya in "Fiddler on the Roof" singing "Lechaim! (To Life!)," then back off one-half an expectoration and you're there: Beth-le-khkhem!

Everyone agrees that Jesus's mother was a Jew named Mary, and Christians believe she got pregnant without any help from a man. In fact, Christians believe God in heaven made Mary pregnant and was the literal father of Jesus.

In the Bible story, a Jew named Joseph later marries Mary and raises Jesus as his own son. Christians believe that Joseph, Mary, and the baby Jesus spent the night of his birth in a barn surrounded by animals, and that Jesus slept in a trough animals ate from, known as a manger. The Christmas holiday is a celebration of the birth of Jesus.

There is a supreme irony in the modern controversy over the secularization of Christmas as seen in modern marketing trends utilizing safe phrases like "Seasons Greetings" or "Happy Holidays." That is, to some paradoxical extent the prominence of Christmas in the modern church calendar was brought on exactly by the secular popularization of the Christmas holiday under commercial marketing schemes like Coca-Cola's famous Saint Nick. In traditional theology, Christmas never meant nearly as much in the church calendar as, say, Easter or even Pentecost, and early Christians associated lavish birthday observances with the self-aggrandizing of hated Roman Caesars. That modern church goers are nonetheless obsessed with Christmas is an annual source of angst to many pastors, priests, and reverends which they delicately and discreetly keep to themselves, in part because Christmas contributions are an end-of-fiscal-year budget "savior" for many, many churches.

In both Biblical accounts of Jesus's birth, a lot is made of how Jewish prophets had for thousands of years predicted his birth, life, and death. It's hard to understand why these predictions would make any difference to Christians today, thousands of years later, since their predecessors long ago ignored the clear instructions of Jesus and abandoned all loyalty to Jewish orthodoxy. Today there may be only a few thousand Jews on the entire planet who believe Jesus was the actual Messiah of Jewish prophecy. And although the narratives in the books of Matthew and Luke go to extreme, dubious lengths to place Jesus's birth in Bethlehem, thereby linking him to King David, Jesus himself, in Matthew Chapter 22, angrily mocked the idea to Pharisees, bragging that if even King David referred to the Messiah as "Lord," how could he be a son of David?

This passage from Matthew closes by stating that "no one was able to answer him a word, nor from that day did any one dare to ask him any more questions."

Christians believe that the baby Jesus received visitors in the barn where he was born, local shepherds sent by angels and so-called Wise Men from the East, who were astronomers from Persia, which we know today as Iran. According to tradition, an unusual star in the sky led these astronomers to Bethlehem, which they thought meant Jesus would be a future king. They came bearing the first Christmas gifts.

If you want to try an interesting experiment, go outside on a clear night, pick out a star high enough in the sky to be visible from a few countries over (hint: any of them will do), then drive or ride a camel to the exact spot beneath it. It's not easy to do (hint: it's impossible).

Among other inconsistencies between the two stories, the shepherds appear only in Luke, and the so-called Wise Men appear only in Matthew. Fortunately, these two groups finally found each other inside snow globes, on the faces of Christmas cards, and in the town square crèches (live nativity scene re-enactments) that give ACLU lawyers something to do every winter.

Only one additional story about Jesus's childhood appears in the Bible, in the book of Luke. Beyond that, we know almost nothing about his life until the last few years of it. And what we do know about those years comes almost exclusively from a total of four books known as the four Gospels, written by four different authors traditionally identified as Matthew, Mark, Luke, and John. The four books are known by the names of these four followers of Jesus despite the fact that almost no one, not even faithful Christian scholars, really believes they were the four actual authors.

The term gospel comes from the Old English phrase "god spell" meaning "good news" or "glad tidings." This term was popularized by the 1971 Broadway play Godspell, which included the Billboard top twenty hit song "Day by Day," a truly snappy little number.

The oldest of these four books, the Gospel of Mark, was written sometime just before the destruction by the Romans of the Jewish capital city of Jerusalem in the year 70 A.D., or about forty years after Jesus's death. Most researchers believe an anonymous author in Rome wrote Mark based on the teachings of Simon Peter, one of the main followers of Jesus before his crucifixion and an early leader in the brand-new Christian faith afterwards.

It is mind-boggling to consider that Christianity had no written record of the life and teachings of Jesus that we know of for such a long period——forty years. That's an entire generation!

Matthew and Luke were both written fifteen to twenty years after Mark, meaning more than fifty years after Jesus's death. The story told in both books seems to be based mainly on Mark. These three gospels—Mark, Matthew and Luke—are so closely related that they are often called "The Synoptic Gospels," meaning they can be laid side-by-side for easy comparison of their many similarities.

As closely related as Matthew and Luke are to Mark, there are some differences. Because these passages in Matthew and Luke which differ from Mark often seem to match each other, researchers believe they came from a common source book of the sayings of Jesus that was *not* available to the author of Mark, but shared by the authors of Matthew and Luke those fifteen to twenty years later. Biblical historians call this book *Quelle* (or just Q for short), which is German for "source." Some scholars believe Q was written around 50 A.D., or about twenty years after Jesus's death.

Wouldn't it be nice to discover a surviving copy of Q that we could consult and compare with the four gospels?

The Gospel of Luke is notable for a couple reasons. For one thing, some people believe it was written by a Gentile (non-Jew) physician during a period when Christianity was quickly spreading to the non-Jewish world, or at least the world outside of Jerusalem. It also contains a story from Jesus's adolescence: at twelve years old he reportedly amazed local priests with his knowledge of sacred Jewish writings. More important, Luke has a companion book, likely written by the same author, called Acts of the Apostles, which provides many insights into the nature of the early Christian Church following Jesus's crucifixion.

The fourth gospel, known as John, was written around twenty years after Matthew and Luke—so maybe forty years after Mark and more than one hundred years after the birth of Jesus. It is written in a much different style from the Synoptic Gospels and contains a wide variety of stories not found in the other three. The Gospel of John also omits a number of important events described in those first three gospels. Among the missing stories are:

- Satan tempting Jesus in the desert,

- The Sermon on the Mount, Jesus's most famous speech by far, and

- The Last Supper, Jesus's final meal.

The Gospel of John contains almost none of the parables (colorful similes Jesus uses to teach his followers) that are so common to the first three gospels, nor is there any mention of The Lord's Prayer, the "Our Father" prayer which is the most famous of all Christian communications with God.

The Christian sign often seen at sporting events, "John 3:16," refers to a popular quotation from the Gospel of John, some might even call it a capsule summary of the Christian message: "For God so loved the world, that he gave his only begotten Son, that whosoever believeth in him should not perish, but have everlasting life."

John is so vastly different from the other three gospels that it might as well be wearing a rainbow wig like that famous John 3:16 sign-waver guy.

These differences point out a surprising fact with regard to the four gospels—the four books on which literally all of Christianity is founded. This may sound unbelievable to non-Christians, but it is well beyond any reasonable dispute: with only a few very minor exceptions, they are the only known sources of information about Jesus, yet these four books *do not agree with each other.* The Christian Church has devised a way over the years to read these books as consistent with one another (or at least consistent enough), but the fact is they repeatedly clash and contradict each other in very important ways. How you think about that clash largely depends on whether you are a believer or nonbeliever.

From a rationalist point of view, this puts Christianity ahead of belief in the Tooth Fairy, which can cite no sacred texts in its support, but behind Pastafarianism, a farcical religion dreamt up by an inspired individual who opposed the teaching of intelligent design theory in the Kansas school system. Its singular Gospel of the Flying Spaghetti Monster stands uniform and free of contradictions.

In January of 2014, a brave local elected official in Chautauqua County, New York took the oath of office while wearing a colander on his head as a Pastafarian "statement about religious freedom."

One thing is certain: no matter how you look at them, it is impossible to overstate the importance to Christianity of the four gospels. Virtually the entire religion is based on the events and teachings described in Matthew, Mark, Luke, and John. Other parts of the Bible serve mainly to expound on those events and teachings or to provide historical background.

It is interesting to consider how much different things would be today had there been newspapers, television, and the Internet during the time of Jesus, or had there been just a single person following him around, making notes of everything he said as he said it. But that didn't happen, so we have to do the best we can to figure it all out from those four gospels, written by unknown authors anywhere from forty to seventy-five years after Jesus died.

Those first writings about Jesus, made from distant memory or hear-say and written with crude lamp-black ink on treated animal skins or papyrus, were doubtless in high demand back then, a feature of this newfangled Christian religion that everybody wanted to read (or at least have read to them, if, like most people during that period, they were illiterate). So it is certain that, right from the start, these books were copied a lot. Shockingly, today we have *no* originals of *any* of the books of the Bible. *None*, not a single one.

This is undoubtedly the sense in which most early Christians "read" the Bible. This tradition is still present in the modern Christian worship service, which typically features at least one reading from the New Testament epistles (letters), and another from one of the four gospels.

Copying back then was all done by hand. Printed books didn't come along until 1455 A.D., when Johann Gutenberg, the inventor of the printing press, produced his first book. Unsurprisingly, it was a Christian Bible.

If you have ever held a Bible, you can appreciate how hard it would be to copy every last word of it by hand. Yet that is exactly how copies of its contents were made for around 1400 years. Unfortunately, the people who did the copying were often *not* professional copyists, especially early in Church history, and in some cases *they could not even read.*

The King James Version of the Christian Bible has close to eight hundred thousand words in it, roughly two hundred thousand more than Leo Tolstoy's notoriously long War and Peace.

It is pretty easy to see how copying errors might have been made under the circumstances. Even so, most experts, including nonbelievers, agree that the Bible was copied pretty accurately for that entire period. This is not good enough for some Christians, who still insist on believing that no mistakes appear anywhere in the Bible. Other Christians believe that it is silly to make such a big deal out of this and are happy and feel fortunate just to have the Bible they have.

A partial listing of Biblical contradictions and likely copying errors (or deliberate changes) appears later in this book.

This idea that God would never allow a mistake to creep into the Bible, called biblical inerrancy, has needlessly caused a great many institutional arguments, or schisms, within Christianity. The logic of this is hard for outsiders to fathom. For example, if God would not allow a copying error, why would God allow a copying controversy? And if inconsistent reporting renders a historical event fictitious, as proponents of inerrancy seem to fear, then it presumably follows that no one is responsible for flying two jet planes into the World Trade Center on September 11, 2001 and no one shot President John F. Kennedy.

The irony is that nowhere in the Christian Bible does it declare itself inerrant or flawless. In fact, the Bible never even mentions itself. What's more, none of the authors of the Bible knew anything about it, or had ever heard of it. Why not? Because by the time the Bible that we know was finally pieced together (to mixed reviews) in the late fourth century, every last one of its authors had been dead for centuries, if not millennia.

Putting aside for the moment how you look at this issue of mistakes in the Bible, what comes next is the story of those few years in the life of Jesus of Nazareth that *were* described in the Bible. Just keep in mind that there are many little differences—and a few big ones—between the versions of Jesus's story found in the four gospels.

Everyone first needs to understand that Jesus lived during the time of the Roman Empire, when Romans controlled much of Europe, North Africa, and the Middle East. That included the place where Jesus lived and taught, which was part of a larger occupied region known by the Romans as Palestine. It encompassed modern-day Palestine, plus Israel and parts of Syria, Lebanon, and Jordan, as we know them today.

Today Rome is the capital of Italy and the location of the Vatican, the sovereign city-state that serves as the headquarters of the Roman Catholic Church.

Roman Palestine was the crossroads of many different cultures, and a dizzying variety of religions swirled all around it. In spite of this, the Jews were determined to hold onto their religious and cultural identity, and they convinced the Romans to grudgingly accept many of their traditions and religious practices.

The Romans even cooperated in the reconstruction of the Jewish Temple at Jerusalem in the time of Jesus, but they forced their way into the daily business of the Temple in a manner that was offensive to many traditionalist Jews. This strange bedfellows arrangement faced no criticism from wealthy Jewish officials, however, whose lucrative positions were well protected by a Roman military presence in the Temple.

Nonetheless, many working-class Jews in those days were fed up with Roman rule, and dreaming of a new Jewish leader who could lead them in a rebellion against the Roman occupiers and a return to national independence.

By 30-35 A.D. or so when Jesus was preaching his message, the Jews had already lived under Roman occupation for going on one hundred years.

Now that you know the background, you should understand that if people in ancient Palestine referred to Jesus of Nazareth as Jesus Christ, the "Christ" part undoubtedly meant, one hundred percent for certain, that they were talking about a paramilitary leader who would help the Jews defeat the Romans in a war of independence, *and absolutely nothing else, period.* Another name for Christ was the Messiah, or chosen one. Only much later, long after Jesus's death, did these terms take on the meanings we now associate with them. There were a number of would-be Messiahs in those times, some self-proclaimed and others by reputation. Most of them were eventually executed by the Romans, Jesus included.

Believe it or not, in 2013 a judge in Tennessee changed the name of an African-American baby from Messiah to Martin against its parents' wishes, saying the former name might offend local residents. This occurred despite the fact that literally millions of people around the world are named Jesus, around 200,000 of them in the United States alone. The ruling of the judge, who was white, was reversed on appeal.

As it turned out, Jesus was no army general. He was an inspirational figure who taught, among other things, that you should love all people, even your worst enemies, and treat them the way you'd like to be treated yourself. Christians today nonetheless believe that Jesus was the chosen one, but consider him chosen by God to give his believers the gifts of forgiveness for their wrongdoing and heavenly life after death. This idea, it must be said, appears *nowhere* in Jewish prophecy or tradition.

Christians have an uncanny knack for shelving some of these more difficult concepts from the teachings of Jesus when they prove inconvenient.

Before any of the four gospels goes very far into the story of Jesus the inspirational teacher and healer, each takes some time to talk about another holy man from that era and region named John the Baptist. John was a devout Jew who lived in the wilderness as part of his spiritual journey of self-denial, meditation, and prayer. He wore animal skins for clothing, and was said to survive by eating locusts* and wild honey. In other words he was an ascetic (a monk of sorts) whom you might compare to a mystical seer.

Many historians believe John, identified in the Gospel of Luke as a distant cousin of Jesus, was a member of the ascetic group known as the Essenes, who lived in the wild country outside Jerusalem in Jesus's time to protest the corruption of the Jewish Temple in the city.

*Unlike most insects, locusts are kosher according to the book of Leviticus. Who knew?

The Dead Sea Scrolls, ancient writings found in a cave at Qumran in modern-day Palestine in the late 1940s and early 1950s, were part of a library created there by the Essenes. Bedouin goatherds reportedly made the initial discovery while searching for a lost goat.

John was widely-known in that region as a spiritual teacher. His message emphasized repentance (that is, apology for wrongdoing), modesty, and generosity, among other virtues. To initiate his followers he would immerse them in the Jordan River. This ritual was and is known as baptism. Jesus's story is rightly said to start when he was baptized by John. According to three of the four gospels, Jesus's baptism was accompanied by a miraculous sign in the sky from God indicating his approval of Jesus, whom he supposedly referred to as his "beloved Son."

The spirit of God that appeared at the scene of Jesus's baptism reportedly took the form of a dove, which remains an important Christian symbol to this day.

In all four gospels the relationship between Jesus and John the Baptist is described in very emotional terms. And though Christians don't always agree one hundred percent about the precise meaning of baptism, or the best way to perform one, they all agree it is one of the most important rites or ceremonies in Christianity.

Some Christians perform baptisms on infants and others only on adults. For some believers baptism seems to be the central focus of their entire worship experience.

The story of John the Baptist ends badly. John was critical of an important woman, Herodias, for marrying Antipas, the ruler of that part of Judea and son of King Herod the Great. The problem was that Herodias was still married at the time to Antipas's brother, Herod's other son (also named Herod). Herodias asked Antipas for John's severed head on a platter, so the story goes, and she got it. The rest of us got a cliché that has survived to this day.

Herodias supposedly had her sultry, young daughter, Salome, perform an erotic dance for Antipas, who was so titillated he granted her a wish —anything she wanted, even half of his kingdom. At her mother's urging, she chose revenge against John instead.

Another aspect of John the Baptist's story is its heavy emphasis on the Christian notion that ancient Jewish scriptures (sacred writings) prophesied or foretold John's announcement of the beginning of Jesus's career.

In this way it is reminiscent of the prophecy-laden story of Jesus's birth. It's very hard to understand why these prophecies still matter so much to Christians, most of whom no longer seek validation from Jewish tradition, and just that easy to understand why they matter so little to Jews, who don't believe in Jesus and therefore couldn't possibly care less.

After his baptism Jesus's next move was to go into the wilderness to meditate, fast, and pray for forty days.

You will notice as you read the Bible that the authors seem fixated on certain numbers, especially the numbers three, four, seven, ten, twelve, and here forty, among others. If that sounds like a winning Powerball ticket to you, well, you can't win if you don't play.

While Jesus was out in the wilderness, so the story goes, Satan came to tempt him. It is impossible to know, but interesting to consider, whether the devil went to Jesus on his own or was in some sense sent by God to test Jesus's readiness.

There are many situations in the Bible (not to mention in real life) where, in retrospect, it seems as if Satan was doing God's work, either intentionally or unwittingly. This is one of them.

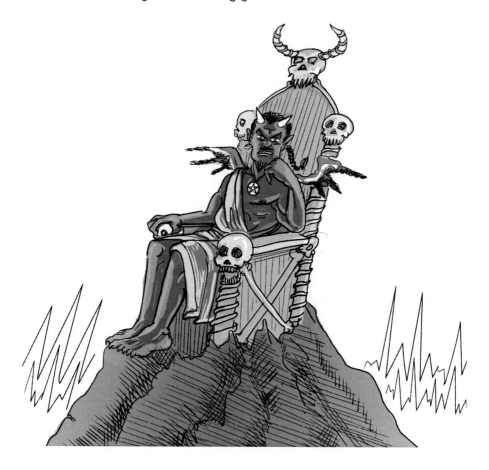

According to the story, Satan tried three times to win Jesus over, tempting him with food, riches, and power, and each time Jesus said no. In the story, Satan put on a dazzling display of supernatural powers while Jesus showed none; he instead seemed simply to be going along for the ride.

When Jesus went back to Galilee he began his mission, so to speak, by recruiting followers, or disciples. They came mostly from among the uneducated and included folks such as fishermen, farmers, laborers, and a very surprising (for that era) number of women featuring prominently among them.

If Jesus came back today, it seems he would have a number of IRS agents as disciples, given that there were quite a few tax collectors among his followers.

According to the Bible, this is also when Jesus started to show that he too had supernatural powers, doing miracles such as healing sick people, exorcizing demons, and reading minds. In a miraculous display sure to please his many fishermen friends, he supposedly caused a large number of fish to swim into their nets.

In the Gospel of John, and only in John, Jesus's first miracle was to turn water into wine for a wedding reception that had run out of alcohol. Unlike an exorcism, such a miracle would be equally useful today.

For the Jews of that period who were watching and waiting for a
Messiah general to help them drive out the Roman occupiers, tales of
Jesus's miracles were clearly important signs that he might be the chosen
one of Yahweh, the god of the Jews. But what made it so confusing was
that he was far from the only charismatic figure doing miraculous signs
in those days.

It's not at all clear why the stories of these miracles, which were important signs to the powerless and despondent Jews of two thousand years ago, remain so important to Christians today. The heart of Christian belief is obviously *not* that Jesus could perform feats of magic or exorcise demons. It is the idea that he triumphed over death, and in so doing provided a free gift to his believers of forgiveness for their wrongdoing, plus their own peaceful life after death. Jesus was critical of belief based solely on the witnessing of miracles, stating in chapter twenty of John, "Have you believed because you have seen me? Blessed are those who have not seen and yet believe."

Nevertheless, to this day the single most compelling aspect of Jesus's story for hundreds of millions of Christians is the notion that he could perform miracles, which is hard to fathom given that several of his rivals are portrayed in the Bible as likewise being capable of miraculous feats (to say nothing of the countless other mythical figures of history said to have supernatural powers). To modern outside observers, the most powerful aspect of Jesus's story is, or at least ought to be, the substance of his revolutionary teaching. Yet the unhealthy Christian fixation on magical thinking and the superiority of Jesus's magic remains strong.

The so-called Thomas Jefferson Bible, which was distributed at government expense to all new U.S. congressmen from 1901 until the 1950s, was created when the third U.S. president literally cut and patched together with razor and glue a version of Jesus's life story and philosophy stripped of all references to supernatural events. In an October 13, 1813 letter to John Adams he compared this process to mining "diamonds in a dunghill."

The real miracle was that Jefferson accomplished this feat two hundred years before the invention of the word processor!

After Jesus assembled a group of followers, he started traveling around Galilee, teaching and healing. In those days, Galilee had a reputation for being a kind of maverick place not always in step with the Jewish leaders in Jerusalem. Even before Jesus arrived on the scene, other charismatic figures from the area had spoken out forcefully against both Roman imperial rule and the conduct of affairs at the Jewish Temple in Jerusalem (which was a comfortable distance away).

You could say that Jesus, being a Galilean, came from the wrong side of the railroad tracks.

At first Jesus's ministry was met with a measure of doubt. In his own hometown of Nazareth, skeptics who knew him personally chose to make fun of him, leading Jesus to famously state that "a prophet is not without honor except in his own country and in his own house" (Matthew 13:57). Right from the beginning he infuriated Jewish officials in Nazareth, who, according to Luke, ran him out of town and actually tried to throw him off a cliff. He managed to escape mysteriously.

Because of the locals' negative attitude, Jesus reportedly performed few or no miracles in his hometown.

This escape from Nazarene officials was the first of a number of times Jesus showed an unexplained ability to slip away from authorities and go into hiding. This recurring spy-like behavior is known among biblical scholars as the Messianic Secret.

Perhaps because of the hostility his hometown people showed, Jesus spent a far greater amount of time teaching and supposedly performing signs in and around Capernaum, a smallish fishing village on the shores of the Sea of Galilee, a walk of several days to the northeast of Nazareth.

However, according to Mark, Matthew and Luke, it was still much too early for Jesus even to think about making the long walk to Jerusalem, where his destiny awaited him.

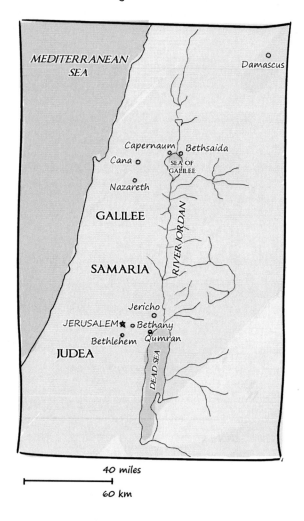

According to three of the four gospels, Jesus soon gained a reputation for teaching in an unusual way, using a lot of parables or similes in his message. This metaphorical style (for example, "The kingdom of heaven is like treasure hidden in a field") confused even his closest followers, who at first had to ask Jesus repeatedly for spoon-fed explanations. Christians today have gotten used to it.

Jesus basically apologized to his followers for this trait several times in the gospels.

It wasn't long after Jesus "came out" (his words) that he gave his most famous and, to most observers, greatest public speech, the so-called Sermon on the Mount, contained in the Gospel of Matthew, chapters five through seven (a shorter, somewhat different version appears in chapter six of Luke). This best-known sermon is perhaps the reason Matthew was positioned first in the eventual collection of books of the so-called New Testament of the Bible. It includes the beatitudes ("blessed are the meek," "...the merciful," "...the peacemakers"); the so-called antitheses ("you have heard...but I say"); and a healthy dose of warnings about the dangers of public piety, materialism, and vanity ("consider the lilies"); along with a recitation of what is known as the Lord's Prayer, still used by Christians today as the first and best way to pray to their god.

Jesus gave other inspirational speeches during this period in Galilee, but none quite as famous or well-loved as the Sermon on the Mount. Because this sermon appears in Matthew and Luke but not Mark, most scholars believe it came from the mysterious Q document described earlier.

Of course, as mentioned before, Jesus also gained a large following during this period because of the miraculous healings and exorcisms he was said to be performing. His fame was growing, as was the resentment of Jewish authority figures for his anti-establishment message.

If you can believe the four gospels, in those days Jesus was casting out more evil spirits than The Ghostbusters.

Jesus was also deputizing some of his followers to teach his message around Galilee and empowering them to perform healings and exorcisms in his name. They later returned to report that they'd been mostly successful in their endeavors.

The teachings of Jesus at this stage of his ministry sound abstract and vaguely apocalyptic to readers today but were undoubtedly perceived much differently in his day, most likely as instructions to prepare right then and there for an imminent war for Jewish independence and subsequent strict Jewish rule.

Another important event that preceded Jesus's fateful trip to Jerusalem was a mountaintop interlude between him and Yahweh, a kind of battery-charging episode known as the Transfiguration. The three Synoptic Gospels describe it in almost identical terms, stating that Moses, who received the Ten Commandments in Jewish lore, and Elijah, an extremely important bygone Jewish prophet, met with Jesus and Yahweh, while Peter, James, and John waited and watched.

It is far from clear how Peter and the others were able to recognize the two guests as Moses and Elijah.

As the mountaintop meeting came to its climax, say the gospels, Jesus turned white with energy, and at the end he received a sort of stamp of approval from God very similar to what occurred in the story of his baptism by John. And then *poof*, all of a sudden Jesus was standing there with just his three disciples.

Jesus's message during this period of evangelism (public teaching with the purpose of conversion) is probably too complicated to summarize briefly. But as you might've guessed, that's exactly what I will now try to do.

The next sound you hear will be the heads of millions of Christians, exploding...

First, it is probably fair to say that Jesus spent more time preaching about righteousness, or right behavior, than anything else. This will come as no surprise to anyone familiar with Christians, who often seem determined to imitate him in this regard by criticizing the behavior of everyone around them on moral grounds, particularly non-Christians. However, the right behavior about which Jesus endlessly lectured *cannot possibly* be understood as anything other than strict adherence to Jewish Law under the Torah, not right behavior as we might understand it today. Back in that time (two thousand years ago), in that place (Galilee), among those people (Jews), there was simply no reference point for right behavior other than Jewish orthodoxy, period.

The principal concern of Jewish orthodoxy in the exact time and place of Jesus was, more than anything else, the elimination of corruption among leading religious figures, which would also be a great focal point for Christians today.

A second theme, connected to the first, that Jesus visited over and over was the evil represented by money and greed. Money, money, money—Jesus never stopped preaching about the evils of it. And he taught not in an ambiguous way, but in a damning, no-holds-barred way. If you sit down and read the four gospels straight through for the first time, which you can do in a few days, you cannot help but feel a kind of rage building inside you over the monstrous hypocrisy of the modern Christian Church. Why, exactly? Because of the way it ignores this constant stream of criticism straight from the mouth of Jesus and aimed directly at wealth, the wealthy, and the corrupting influence of money, *especially* in the church.

According to Jesus, "It is easier for a camel to go through the eye of a needle than for a rich man to enter the Kingdom of Heaven" (Mark 10:25).

Which brings us to a third subject, which should be equally as embarrassing to modern Christians as the first two, seeing as how they 1) would make terrible Jews, and 2) often seem obsessed with the accumulation, preservation, and garish display of wealth.

Hypocrisy, that least-talked-about theme of Jesus's teachings, was without a doubt one of his favorites. He almost constantly railed against different forms of hypocrisy, perpetrated not by the common man, but by prominent religious leaders. If we can say that Jesus identified in his teachings a sin not previously found in religious instruction, it is this sin of hypocrisy, of holier-than-thou self-righteousness.

Could anyone in his or her right mind who has carefully read the New Testament of the Christian Bible possibly believe that Jesus would approve of the sanctimonious attitudes and hypocritical conduct of prominent Christians today?

Could this summary of the teachings of Jesus get any worse for modern Christians? Well, yes, it could. Because another of Jesus's favorite themes—also a favorite of his mentor and predecessor John the Baptist—was humility. And how could even the most forgiving description of modern Christians, one that gave them credit for their frequent good intentions, their generous charity work, their slavish devotion to their church communities, and their dedication to a wide variety of other laudable Christian principles, possibly credit them with anything even approaching the kind of humility taught by John the Baptist and Jesus?

There is an amusing story in the gospels featuring several of Jesus's apostles, whom you could describe as his top lieutenants, arguing over which of them was the first and best apostle. It was a tough question, as all were righteous and had given up everything to follow him. Jesus condemned the whole concept and dismissively declared the least of them the best.

There were other themes in his teaching, including notably the concept of the Kingdom of God. It is difficult today to know for certain exactly what Jesus meant by those teachings, but it's not at all difficult to imagine how his listeners received them. For starters, we can rule out the approach of modern Christians. *Jewish history and prophecy contained absolutely nothing even remotely resembling a Jewish Messiah who would die and be resurrected to provide believers with forgiveness for their sins and life after death.* You can look it up, as they say. So for those lucky enough to hear Jesus preach in person, their only possible understanding of his message was in terms of a new earthly Jewish kingdom free from Roman rule, or for those inclined toward the supernatural, perhaps in terms of a Jewish-themed apocalypse soon to come.

Modern Christology, or how Christians understand the meaning of Jesus's life, death, and resurrection in their belief system, was for the most part first developed during the decades following his crucifixion in the letters of Saint Paul. These letters (or epistles), plus the four gospels and the book of Acts, are the most important parts of the Christian Bible. Paul never met Jesus in person, but claimed to have had supernatural private conversations with him on a regular basis.

Time and again in his teachings, Jesus emphasized strict adherence to *Jewish* Law. Once again, that is something modern Christians could never hope to achieve, or even want to achieve. Jewish Law involved many, many things that would sound crazy today, such as complex dietary restrictions and purification rituals, or downright barbaric, such as the frequent ritual sacrifice of animals.

Although Jesus spoke often of strict adherence to Jewish Law, the truth is that at times his actions told a different story. On a number of occasions he was caught breaking the Sabbath, the Jewish custom of doing no work on the last day of the week. He responded to his critics defiantly, calling himself "Lord of the Sabbath" and stating that this religious custom should serve mankind, not the other way around. He and his followers were also criticized for lax adherence to Jewish cleanliness customs and a general lack of piety.

Just before that conversation, Jesus addressed critics who claimed among other things that he and his men drank a lot. He rebuffed the criticism, but without denying the factual basis for it (Matthew 11:18–19). Recall that his first miracle (according to John at least) was to extend the revelry following the wedding at Cana by turning water into wine.

On the other hand, in the so-called antitheses of his Sermon on the Mount ("You have heard that it was said…but I say…") he mostly called for *strengthening* Jewish law, not relaxing it. Either way, if you take Jesus at his word, there can be little doubt about where he stood on its importance. In chapter five of Matthew he said "Until heaven and earth pass away, not an iota, not a dot, will pass from the [Jewish] law."

In the so-called antitheses, Jesus very clearly took the mind-blowing position that mere violent thoughts make one a murderer, and mere adulterous thoughts make one an adulterer. By this standard we are all probably doomed.

This is as good a place as any to note several of the more serious differences between how the first three Synoptic Gospels describe this period of Jesus's life and the story told in the Gospel of John, the last and most unusual of the four.

Note: If you are a Christian who cannot stand to think about the Bible having contradictions in it, this would be a good time to put up your deflector shields and batten down the hatches.

For starters, in the first three Synoptic Gospels this whole period of ministry in and around Galilee can be seen as the dramatic lead-up to Jesus's climactic journey to Jerusalem, where he would initially be welcomed as the people's champion, but ultimately be seized, tried, tortured, and crucified.

If this were the screenplay for a cowboy Western, the trip to Jerusalem would be the inevitable showdown with the rival gunslinger.

In John, however, Jesus made not one preliminary trip to Jerusalem, but *two*. And they weren't insignificant. During the first, Jesus went publicly crazy in the main Jewish Temple and threw out all the animal vendors and money changers. During the second he famously cured a cripple struggling to get in the healing bubble pool at Beth-za'tha (or Bethesda) in time for it to work its magic. These early trips to the big city in John are simply impossible to reconcile with the other three gospels.

In case you ever wondered, this is why everywhere you look there are hospitals named Bethesda.

John also contains arguably the most poetic rendition of Jesus's message (some might say the most grandiose and off-putting). In John, both Jesus and the author speak in soaring metaphors of how Jesus was "living water," "the bread of life," "the way, the truth, and the life," and "the good shepherd." It also contains a number of contrasting images from the thought-world of the increasingly Greek-influenced era of Christianity when it was written (around 100 A.D.), dualistic notions such as light/darkness, truth/lies, and love/hatred.

And any discussion of John would be incomplete without mentioning that it is here that the evolution of Jesus, so to speak, reaches its conclusion, going from the failed earthly Jewish Messiah of Roman history to the rehabilitated divine cosmic Messiah of the Synoptic Gospels to John's vision of a literal god-man who, along with God the Father and a third party whom Christians call the Holy Spirit (or Holy Ghost), would ultimately be considered one-third of a triple, or triune, God.

John drives this point home right from its first sentence—"En arche en ho Logos," Greek for "In the beginning was the Word." Logos/ the Word was John's designation for Jesus the god-man, who is said to have existed before time itself and was therefore present at the creation of the world.

The metaphysical use of the term logos had, in the time of Jesus, already been a feature of Greek philosophy for hundreds of years.

This was all part of the Christology developing toward the end of the first century, the process of figuring out just what Jesus's life story meant, referenced earlier. After all, early Christians were starting from scratch, there was no Bible, and the many claims of seeing Jesus and talking to him resurrected and in the flesh had mostly petered out by 100 A.D.

One theme was constant in early Christian literature, and even implicit in some outside documentary evidence: a significant number of early Christians claimed to have seen Jesus resurrected, and they were determined to stick to their story even if they had to die for it.

The important differences between John and the other three gospels start but don't stop with Christology. As mentioned earlier, John contains no birth story for Jesus and nothing about his childhood; there is no mention of his temptation by Satan in the desert; Jesus did not use his trademark parables (or similes) to teach his message to the simple folks of Galilee; his famous Sermon on the Mount speech from Q is conspicuously absent; he did not teach his followers the Lord's Prayer; and last but not least, there is no Last Supper, the crucial final meal of Jesus that formed the model for Christian Holy Communion.

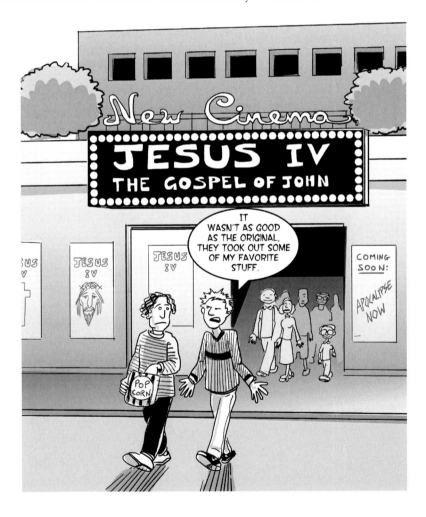

This meal, also known as the Holy Eucharist, is a vitally important Christian worship ritual that recalls the Jewish Passover meal Jesus ate the night before he died. In it the Jewish unleavened flat bread (or matzo) is supposed to represent the body of Jesus, and the red wine his blood. Christians *do not* all agree about the details, as there is much argument, strangely, about whether the meal is symbolic or whether the body and blood of Jesus are *actually and literally present in the bread and wine.*

Scientists agree they are not present.

But we are getting ahead of ourselves. Before Jesus could have that last meal, he had to make a fateful trip to Jerusalem, and in all four gospels that's exactly what he did. The purpose of the trip in all four gospels was to celebrate the Jewish Passover holiday at the Jewish Temple in the Jewish capital.

The four versions of his journey contain a number of similarities as well as some important differences. For example, in all three Synoptic Gospels, Jesus paused before he left for Jerusalem to cite the modesty and innocence of children as a worthy example for Christians to follow. *Jesus obviously never met the children in my extended family!*

You will find that many obtuse Fundamentalists like to divert adult intellectual discourse on the serious matters discussed in this book by reference to these passages on children. But not only is this a disgraceful refusal to make full use of what is, using their jargon, "God's greatest gift to them," their superior human brain (the most complex on Earth), it is probably a misinterpretation of what Jesus actually meant. He never once spoke about the "faith" of a child. Jesus was not holding up children as some kind of model of gullibility worthy of following. In Mark and Luke in particular it seems clear from the context that he was praising them for their humility and openness, which modern Christians would indeed do well to imitate.

The list of child-like traits we could all stand to mimic is long: humility, openness to new things, playfulness, colorblindness, sensitivity to others' feelings, willingness to forgive and forget, ability to live in the moment, and there are many, many more. The faith or trust of a child is by any standard precious, but in truth it is neither hard won nor the least bit reliable, and it is often abused. Surely the one thing Christians and non-Christians can all agree on is that if there is a literal hell, it was made for the villains who abuse this trust and harm innocent children.

In all four gospels, Jesus repeatedly ruined the mood on the road to Jerusalem with gloomy predictions of his betrayal, capture, torture, and death upon their arrival.

The most dramatic factual differences in this part of the story, as usual, appear in John. It is missing important action sequences, some of which I referenced earlier. For another example, in the three Synoptic Gospels Jesus rode triumphantly into town on the back of an animal and received a hero's welcome. There were revelers waving palm fronds and laying down their cloaks like a red carpet. But not in John.

However, the single most important factual difference might be this: in John, Jesus stopped along the way to raise a man (Lazarus) from the dead, which serves in John's narrative to cement Jesus's place as the greatest of the would-be Messiahs of that time. And in so doing, Jesus convinced Jewish authority figures that he was a threat to Temple authority so grave he had to be taken out, whacked, eliminated.

What is peculiar about this storyline in John—that Jesus signed his own death warrant when he cranked his fame up several notches resurrecting a dead person—is that in the other three gospels he already had at least one resurrection miracle under his belt well before he made the trip to Jerusalem, namely the dead daughter of the synagogue honcho Jairus, as told in Matthew chapter nine, Mark chapter five, and Luke chapter eight.

Also, this act of resurrecting a dead person would, to an outside observer, seem to take some of the luster off Jesus's own subsequent resurrection. These logical inconsistencies seem lost on Christian readers, however.

In the three Synoptic Gospels, Jesus followed his grand entrance into Jerusalem with his notorious episode in the Temple, when he raged and ranted at the moneychangers and salesmen, upsetting their tables, animal cages, and other wares. Recall, however, that in John *this crucial episode took place during a previous visit.*

Much of the worship conducted at the Temple consisted of the ritual sacrifice to Yahweh of select animals (with the help of paid, official assistants) as a form of atonement for wrongdoing. In a crossroads metropolis full of Jewish pilgrims from all over, carrying every different kind of money, these animals had to be purchased with local Hebrew coins (shekels), which is why the place came to resemble both a marketplace and a bank.

Pretty much everyone, believer and nonbeliever alike, agrees this extremely important event in the life story of Jesus was either a historical fact or, at the very least, a plausible theory of what took place during Passover week that year in Jerusalem. It might well have been the exact reason he was crucified. You want to talk about key moments in time? That was the indignant tantrum that changed the course of two thousand years (and counting) of human history!

And speaking of money, as if this story weren't already bad enough for modern, conservative Bible thumpers, Jesus's trip to Jerusalem also included the tale in Matthew chapter twenty-two of him explicitly telling his listeners to shut up and pay their damned taxes with his "render unto Caesar what belongs to Caesar" speech.

The gospels provide another tax episode in which Jesus quieted Peter from whining about a certain Temple levy by having him catch a fish with a one shekel coin in its mouth —enough to pay the tax for both of them (Matthew 17:24-27).

The tough question Jesus deflected with his reference to Caesar's image on the Roman coin was one of several attempts by Temple confederates to trick Jesus into incriminating himself during his stay in Jerusalem. In another, he was asked about the marital status in heaven of widows who, under Jewish law, were forced to copulate with their deceased husbands' brothers until they conceived male heirs (gross, I know). Jesus's answer was fascinating for a couple of reasons. One, he stated pretty clearly that life after death was incorporeal, that one did not precisely maintain one's earthly form or identity. This should be a pretty big deal to those curious about such things. Two, *Jesus in no way criticized this revolting Hebrew practice!* Is it really necessary to look any further than this one story to grasp the utter irrelevance of Biblical sexual mores to society today?

During this period when Jesus was in and around Jerusalem, he also made remarks strongly suggesting that he would return with a vengeance before the last of his followers died, which led many of the earliest Christians to believe they would be alive to witness it.

However, there is no good reason to believe they expected a universal apocalypse of the type envisioned by Christian revenge fetishists like Tim LaHaye in his utterly deranged and unbiblical "Left Behind" series. Most Jews of that period undoubtedly expected something more along the lines of a paramilitary restoration of Jewish self-rule and punishment for their local tormentors, principally the Romans, albeit one perhaps aided by supernatural means.

There were other curious episodes during this prelude to Jesus's cru-cifixion. Two vividly illustrate the profoundly human nature and tem-perament of this man who, in other parts of the Bible, wept and showed fear. In the first, Jesus woke up hungry and tried to eat from a fig tree only to find no figs growing on it. His reaction was to strike the guilty tree dead! In the second, he indulged himself a sensuous foot washing and oiling delivered, apparently, by a prostitute.

But it's not that hard to imagine why a man marked for death, who had spent years practicing extreme self-denial, would permit himself the momentary luxury of a young woman at his feet, washing and oiling him sensuously with her long, wet hair, is it?

Whether inspired by the prostitute or not, Jesus then promptly used the example of foot-washing as a model for humbling oneself before others when he cleaned the feet of his disciples in a touching display for a would-be king. To fully appreciate the significance of this, consider the feet of two thousand years ago, with no running water, no regular bathing, and only primitive sandals for footwear. Recall also that walking was the primary form of transportation back then, and that roads also served as both sewers and garbage dumps.

While the foot-washing ritual remains a minor rite in some Christian circles, it is hard to understand why it is not more front and center, since Jesus demonstrated it more or less in conjunction with the rite of Holy Communion, and it perfectly captures some of the very best aspects of the Christian ethic, namely humility and self-sacrifice.

The Last Supper, which Jesus celebrated during that week in Jerusalem, was a traditional Jewish Passover meal, or Seder, of unleavened bread and wine. It was done in remembrance of the tale of the tenth and final plague Yahweh sent against Egypt to free the enslaved Jewish people in Hebrew lore. This was the plague that killed the first-born male in every non-Jewish household, including the Pharaoh's, and finally resulted in the Jews' release and exodus to the promised land, led, of course, by Moses. Jews marked the occasion then and still do now with a highly ritualized meal featuring flat bread (today called matzo), wine, bitter herbs, and ceremonial hand washing.

The many paintings of the Last Supper produced the surprise benefit of establishing the standard seating arrangement for the traditional TV sitcom meal scene.

Interestingly, Sunni Muslims also celebrate Passover by observing a fast to commemorate Allah's rescue of Moses and his followers from the Egyptian Pharaoh. This once again demonstrates the stunning similarity with which the three Abrahamic faiths (Judaism, Christianity, and Islam) worship notwithstanding their ceaseless fixation on comparatively minor differences.

You might ask —"What is their greatest similarity?" Opinions vary, but surely it is their hair-trigger readiness to hate in the names of their respective gods.

In the years that followed, the ritual of Holy Communion took on increasing importance until it became the centerpiece of most Christian worship. The focal point of Christian churches became the altar table at the front of the sanctuary, where the ritual meal was prepared, blessed, and shared by the congregation. More recently, the model of being a dinner guest in God's house has been replaced by the concept of a God-themed rock concert focused mainly on the M.C. and the various performers. Some services even feature God-themed comedians to warm up the house.

Just kidding, but in some churches you do wonder...

If the macabre idea of remembering the death and resurrection of Jesus by eating bread and drinking wine symbolizing his body and blood is hard for you to wrap your mind around, you are not alone. When Jesus proclaimed in John 6:54 that "he who eats my flesh and drinks my blood has eternal life," his stunned followers responded incredulously: "This is a hard saying; who can listen to it?" The gospel then notes that "after this many of his disciples drew back and no longer went about with him."

At some point during the Last Supper, all three Synoptic Gospels have Jesus accusing one of his twelve apostles of betraying him. The culprit turned out to be Judas Iscariot, who served as treasurer for the group. Judas fled and Jesus went with the remaining eleven for a walk to a nearby garden, called Gethsemane.

Judas reportedly received thirty silver coins for betraying Jesus, but he never got to spend them. According to Matthew, he attempted to return the money to the church figures who had bribed him, then he committed suicide. If you are looking for a better story than that, try the version in chapter one of Acts of the Apostles, the companion book to Luke, where Judas used the money to buy a field, then "swelling up, he burst open in the middle and all his bowels gushed out."

When they reached the Garden of Gethsemane, Jesus and his eleven disciples engaged in a sort of tragic comedy bit wherein Jesus, apparently feeling the tension of his imminent fate, asked them to stay awake with him while he prayed and awaited his arrest. Time and again they instead fell asleep, having just washed down their Passover meals with healthy doses of wine. Reading the story, one can almost picture them snoring like eleven stooges.

Jesus was not pleased, but before any more could come of it, a large group arrived, including some soldiers and Judas the traitor, who infamously pointed out Jesus with a kiss. The always-excitable Simon Peter apparently used a sword to slice off the ear of a member of the group, a slave of the high priest, and Jesus—who either heals the ear or doesn't, depending on which gospel you read—then admonished him with his famous line about he who lives by the sword perishing by the sword.

At Mark 14:51–52 there is an odd reference to a young man fleeing the scene of Jesus's arrest—odd because it also mentions that he did so while naked.

This is the only known incidence of streaking in the New Testament.

From Gethsemane, Jesus was purportedly hauled before Caiaphas, the high priest of the Jewish Temple, on charges of blasphemy (John has him appearing before Ananus, a former high priest, on his way to Caiaphus). In all four gospels the high priest asked him whether he was "the Christ," and in three of them he dodged the question. Only in Mark, the oldest of the four, did he plainly say "I am."

Jewish scholars have pointed out that this sequence of events would have been impossible under then-prevailing Jewish Law, as they were prohibited from convening after dark, particularly during a Temple festival like Passover.

For reasons touched on earlier, this question—"Are you the Christ?"—simply must, from a historical standpoint, be understood *not* to mean "Are you the Son of God sent to die for the forgiveness of sins?" Neither did it mean "Are you the Son of God sent to preside over a Jewish apocalypse?" Nowhere in Jewish tradition does the concept of the literal *Son of God* assuming the form of a man appear. No, no, no. The question logically *had* to mean "Do you claim to be the charismatic military leader of Jewish prophecy, who will, in the tradition of the great King David, lead the Jews to victory over their Roman oppressors, and restore the Kingdom of God (that is, society governed strictly by Jewish Law) to Israel?"

So even though Jesus was not claiming to be part god, he still managed to make the high priest so furious over this blasphemy that he tore his clothing in anger. There is no evidence that he also turned green.

In all four gospels, Jesus was passed from the Jewish high priest to Pontius Pilate, who was in fact verifiably the Roman prefect (like a governor) of Judea (which included Jerusalem) during this period in history. In all four gospels Pilate is described as reluctant to crucify Jesus. He even offered the crowd amnesty for its choice of criminals, Jesus or a notorious criminal named Barabbas. The Jews reportedly picked Barabbas, whereupon a conflicted Pilate "washed his hands" of the matter.

Historians scoff at the idea that Pilate, known as a ruthless disciplinarian, would have been inclined to show mercy to any troublemaker, or that he would risk his relationship with the Jewish high priest because of a hunch about an accused's innocence. That Pilate would crucify a Jew for nothing more than aspiring to be "the Christ" is clear from Roman archival evidence that a number of would-be Christs were executed during this exact historical period, basically for treason or insurrection.

All four gospels report that Jesus was then "scourged" or beaten in preparation for his crucifixion. While there's no historical reason to doubt that a beating took place, neither is there any compelling evidence in the gospels or in history books to support the orgy of torture depicted in the Mel Gibson movie *The Passion of the Christ*.

The scourging scene in The Passion of the Christ could hardly be more pornographic if a dominatrix in a bustier and stiletto heels were delivering the blows.

The four gospels describe the crucifixion of Jesus with alarming variation. He carried his own cross in one version, in three others it was carried for him. In John there is no mention of the individuals crucified near Jesus. In Matthew and Mark, the crucified criminals flanking him for some strange reason went to the trouble of mocking him from their crosses, with their dying breaths. In Luke, by contrast, one of the two criminals saw the light and asked Jesus to forgive him, and Jesus obliged, telling him they'd meet again in Paradise.

This business of dying criminals mocking Jesus from their crosses appears to be one of the earliest known examples of gallows humor.

However, these minor factual differences in how the four gospels describe Jesus's crucifixion are nothing compared to the different demeanors of Jesus seen during the crucifixion ordeal. Starting with the gospels of Matthew and Mark, we see a Jesus who was in a number of ways irritable, anguished by his imminent arrest (and no doubt by its likely outcome). When he went with his disciples to the Garden of Gethsemane, he is described as "greatly distressed and troubled." He said to them "My soul is very sorrowful, even unto death." He *fell* to the ground and prayed. He asked Yahweh two (or three) times to be excused from his fate. He was silent as he went to Mount Golgotha to be crucified. He said nothing from the cross until his dying breath, when he cried *"E'lo-i, E'lo-i, la'ma sabach-tha'ni?"* That is, "My God, my God, why hast thou forsaken me?" In other words, without a trace of hopefulness, Jesus lamented his fate. Then he died.

Although this line is accurately quoted in Gibson's *Passion*, the movie can in no way claim to be faithful to Mark in the details of Jesus's trial and crucifixion, a sequence of events known as the Passion Narrative long before that movie was ever made.

Contrast that with Luke's version of the Passion story, in which Jesus displayed a serene disposition throughout the ordeal, from arrest until his death. There is no mention of his being distressed, troubled, or sorrowful. Rather than falling to the ground to pray in the garden, he simply knelt. When praying, he asked Yahweh only once to "remove this cup from me" (to be excused from his ordeal) but only if Yahweh so wished. He spoke forcefully to onlookers on the path to Mount Golgotha, showing concern for their fate, not his own. He asked Yahweh to forgive the people nailing him to his cross. In short, he was in complete command of his fate, showing total trust in Yahweh throughout. As stated earlier, he engaged in an articulate conversation *from the cross* with the two criminals flanking him, and gracefully forgave the one who asked. Finally, rather than cursing his fate before dying as in Mark, the Jesus of Luke calmly declared "Father, into your hands I commend my spirit," then he peacefully checked out.

Last but not least, and as we have come to expect, no event from the life of Jesus would be complete without the Gospel of John bringing a distinctive new twist to it. As already noted, in John's version Jesus carried his own cross. He stopped along the road to Golgotha and asked his favorite disciple to care for his mother. He said he was thirsty and accepted the drink he refused in Matthew and Mark. There was no conversation with the criminals flanking him. When he died, he simply declared "It is finished." Not only that, but unlike in the other three gospels, in John there is no special-effects showstopper to prove the divinity of Jesus, such as the Temple curtain tearing in two or darkness falling over the land; there is no centurion declaring him innocent or, alternatively, the son of God, and no dead people rise from their tombs to enter the city. Instead there is just the story of how, rather than breaking his legs to ensure his death, the attending soldiers "pierced his side with a spear, and there came out blood and water," supposedly to fulfill yet another prophecy.

Of course, no one but the legendary John Wayne, "The Duke," could have played the Roman centurion at the scene of Jesus's crucifixion in the Hollywood blockbuster The Greatest Story Ever Told.

In all four gospels, a Jewish follower of Jesus named Joseph of Arimathea asks for and receives his dead body and then places it in a new tomb, which Joseph may or may not have owned (again the gospels conflict). John as usual throws in something extra, a role in the burial for the enigmatic Nicodemus, a local Temple figure and secret follower of Jesus.

If you're inclined to believe in such things, the spare bed sheet this Joseph of Arimathea used to wrap Jesus's body was about to become the most famous piece of cloth in Christian history.

But of course, as important as these details of Jesus's crucifixion are, they are nothing compared to the story of his resurrection, the *pièce de résistance* one would expect must *surely* be presented more or less identically in the four gospels. *But*...one would again be disappointed. In fact they don't even come close to matching up (sigh). And, once again, Christians have developed a method, all but incomprehensible to non-Christians, for reading them harmoniously with one another. As much or more than any other aspect of the Bible, these four resurrection stories, to be understood properly, should be considered in chronological order, which means starting with Mark, the oldest of the four gospels.

As always, try to keep the chronological sequence of the four gospels in mind. See the following page for assistance, and don't forget the fundamental fact that Jesus was born around 1 A.D. (though some scholars seem to prefer 4 A.D.) and died thirty-some years later.

MARK was written close to the time that Rome obliterated Jerusalem in 70 A.D., destroying the Temple and slaughtering just about every Jew it could lay hands on, with the rest fleeing to the four corners of the Earth in fear or exile (the so-called Jewish Diaspora). This was when Roman troops chased a particularly stubborn group of Jewish rebels to the impregnable Masada hilltop, where these holdouts famously committed mass suicide rather than surrender.

MATTHEW and **LUKE** came maybe fifteen years later, or around 85 A.D. —well into Christianity's transition from a heretical Jewish sect to a faith more open to non-Jewish believers. They were based mainly on Mark, plus the sayings of Jesus taken from the elusive Q document.

JOHN was probably written just after the turn of the first century, between 100 and 110 A.D., when most of Jesus's contemporaries were surely dead. John marches to the beat of its own drummer, deviating wildly from the other three gospels both factually and in its theology. In John, Judaism has been deemphasized in a number of ways, and the Romans and other Gentiles have been exonerated in a number of ways. For the first time, Jesus is portrayed as not just the Messiah, but *the literal Son of God, present at creation.* In John, Judaism was left far behind, and the transformation of Christianity from an odd and exclusive Jewish cult into a trendy and accessible belief system was in full swing.

Mark has, by far, the shortest and simplest of the four resurrection stories. On the Sunday after Jesus's Friday crucifixion, three women—Mary Magdalene, Mary the mother of James, and Salome—went to his tomb just after sunrise to embalm his body. To their surprise, they found the large stone rolled away from the tomb entrance. They went in and found a young man dressed in a white robe, who told them that Jesus had risen from the dead, and they should inform the others he'd gone ahead of them to Galilee, where he would appear to them. The women fled the tomb, "for trembling and astonishment had come upon them; and they said nothing to anyone, for they were afraid." *And this, according to most Biblical scholars, is precisely where Mark ends, without another word!*

And there you have it. End of story. Mark finishes abruptly with history's only known example of women with amazing news maintaining complete silence about it. But in all seriousness, despite the fact that this authentic version of Mark at least reports Jesus's resurrection from the dead, its ending stands as a staggering anti-climax, to say the least. Do the women *ever* tell the others what they saw? Do the others *ever* encounter Jesus back in Galilee? It's a movie in need of a different ending, which is just what later copyists provided, adding verses nine through twenty to chapter sixteen to tie a tidier bow on top of the story.

Many of the oldest and best surviving manuscripts of Mark end with verse eight. That is, the women run away and tell no one. Not only that, but the additional material in other manuscripts tends to vary, pointing to the conclusion they were altered.

In these additional verses, which even faithful Christian scholars admit show every sign of being a later add-on, Jesus made three appearances: first to Mary Magdalene, then "in another form" (whatever that means) to two other women, then at the dinner table to the remaining eleven disciples, whom he "upbraided" for their unbelief. He then charged them to "go into all the world and preach the gospel to the whole creation. He who believes and is baptized will be saved; but he who does not believe will be condemned." And if this sounds to you suspiciously like the exact rhetoric to end Mark that the young faith would order off a menu, well, you are not alone.

The dubious additional material also includes the gospel's notorious reference to snake-handling and the drinking of poison as proof of sincere belief. One can only wonder how many faithful have died over the centuries in service of this questionable re-write of Mark.

Matthew builds on this tidier version of Mark. First, it makes clear that the tomb was well sealed and guarded by soldiers at the urging of Jewish church officials. On Sunday morning, Mary Magdalene and "the other Mary" (unclear which one, there were several) went to check on Jesus's tomb. As they arrived there was an earthquake, and the large stone sealing the tomb was rolled away. This was the work of an angel dressed in white with the appearance of lightning, who sat atop the stone and told the women not to be afraid. He explained that Jesus was going ahead of them to Galilee, where he would meet them. The story, which up to this point has closely paralleled the original version of Mark, suddenly veers off. The women, terrified and dumbstruck in Mark, instead departed "with fear *and great joy,*" and ran "*to tell his disciples*" (emphasis added).

Jesus then appeared before the women along the way and reminded them to round up his followers and meet him in Galilee. There is a brief description of Jewish officials bribing the soldiers who'd seen the angel to say instead that Jesus's disciples had stolen his body to support their resurrection hoax, which adds that "this story has been spread among the Jews to this day." In other words, Matthew takes a time-out to rebut what must have been in those days a persistent rumor of resurrection fraud.

Matthew closes with Jesus appearing before the eleven remaining disciples on a Galilee mountaintop rather than at the dinner table of (amended) Mark, but it includes a very similar closing commission right out of a church marketing handbook, complete with a hint of support for the embryonic concept of a triple-identity (or triune) multi-god that appears nowhere else in Matthew.

That epilogue, which reads suspiciously like a script, states:

"Go therefore and make disciples of all nations, baptizing them in the name of the Father and of the Son and of the Holy Spirit, teaching them to observe all that I have commanded you; and lo, I am with you always, to the close of the age" (Matthew 28:19-20).

Luke tells yet a third version of the resurrection, but one with a familiar cherry on top. There is no mention of guards, bribes, or earthquakes. The women, identified as Mary Magdalene, Mary the mother of James, and Joanna, were accompanied by "other women." They went to the tomb and found Jesus's body missing, and not one but two men in "dazzling apparel" claiming he was alive. The women left and reported this to the men of their group, who dismissed it as an "idle tale."

That day two other female followers of Jesus were walking to a nearby village when Jesus appeared to them, but for some odd reason they couldn't tell it was him. Later at dinner, Jesus sort of re-enacted the Last Supper with them. They were suddenly able to identify him as Jesus, but in that same moment he vanished. They hurried back to Jerusalem to report what they'd seen, and were told that Simon Peter had also seen Jesus alive. Jesus then suddenly appeared to the group in the flesh, at first startling them, then reassuring them. He asked to eat and received a piece of broiled fish.

This unrecognizability of Jesus is rather bizarre and brings to mind the so-called apocryphal gospels, ancient writings that didn't make the cut for inclusion in the Bible, in which Jesus is sometimes interestingly described as a sort of shape-shifter. Here is an example.

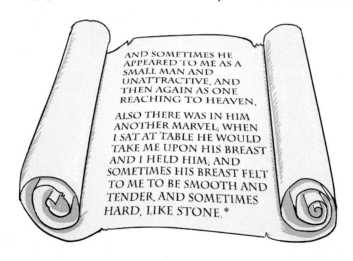

AND SOMETIMES HE APPEARED TO ME AS A SMALL MAN AND UNATTRACTIVE, AND THEN AGAIN AS ONE REACHING TO HEAVEN.

ALSO THERE WAS IN HIM ANOTHER MARVEL: WHEN I SAT AT TABLE HE WOULD TAKE ME UPON HIS BREAST AND I HELD HIM; AND SOMETIMES HIS BREAST FELT TO ME TO BE SMOOTH AND TENDER, AND SOMETIMES HARD, LIKE STONE.*

* THE ACTS OF JOHN, CHAPTER 89

Jesus then spelled out to those present how his death was not an unhappy ending, but in fact necessary to fulfill his destiny, as well as Jewish prophecy. Note that his commentary perfectly tracks the difficult job facing the fledgling church at the time Luke was written: explaining the meaning of Jesus's death to skeptical Jews. The efforts of the young church to reach new, non-Jewish audiences are likewise reflected in Jesus's command to his disciples "that repentance and forgiveness of sins should be preached in his name *to all nations, beginning from Jerusalem*" (emphasis added).

That such marketing strategies, loaded with freshly coined Christian slogans, should close out these later versions of the gospel but not the first of them (the unadulterated Mark) again seems, at the very least, a bit suspicious.

And finally we come to that most eccentric of gospels, the Gospel of **John**. In it Mary Magdalene went alone to the tomb while it was still dark and found the stone rolled away from the entrance. She ran and told Peter and the anonymous "disciple whom Jesus loved," traditionally thought to be John (the gospel's titular author), and all three rushed to the tomb but found it empty. The two men returned home, but Mary stayed, at first crying outside the tomb, then entering to find two "angels" dressed in white. They asked why she was crying, she answered that it was because someone had taken Jesus's body. Then someone standing behind her, who she assumed was the gardener, asked her the same question. Not recognizing him, she pleaded with him to tell her where the body was. He spoke her name, and just like the women in Luke, Mary was suddenly able to recognize the seemingly polymorphous Jesus. He sent her to tell the disciples he was "ascending to my Father and your Father, to my God and your God," which she proceeded to do.

This again brings to mind the descriptions of Jesus which appear in some apocryphal gospels. These accounts were extremely troublesome to early proto-orthodox Christians, who at the time were struggling to ward off competing views of the nature of Jesus that deemed him something other than a true flesh-and-blood human being. The following is another example.

ANOTHER GLORY I WILL TELL YOU, BRETHREN. SOMETIMES WHEN I MEANT TO TOUCH HIM, I MET MATERIAL AND SOLID BODY; AND AT OTHER TIMES AGAIN WHEN I FELT HIM, THE SUBSTANCE WAS IMMATERIAL AND BODILESS AND AS IF IT WERE NOT EXISTING AT ALL.

AND OFTEN WHEN I WAS WALKING WITH HIM I WISHED TO SEE WHETHER THE PRINT OF HIS FOOT APPEARED UPON THE EARTH - FOR I SAW HIM RAISING HIMSELF FROM THE EARTH BUT I NEVER SAW IT. *

* THE ACTS OF JOHN, CHAPTER 93

Later that night, Jesus appeared before his disciples in the shut-up home where they were hiding from Jewish church officials. He breathed on them to give them some of the supernatural powers of the Holy Spirit (or Wind, or Breath), which again was a kind of emerging Christian concept being rolled out in John along with the godhood of Jesus. Thomas, one of his closest followers, was not present, and later said he would never believe until he put his fingers in the nail holes of Jesus's hand. Needless to say, Jesus did return after eight days and showed Thomas his crucifixion injuries, and the nickname "doubting Thomas" was born.

Some biblical historians have wondered aloud if the doubting Thomas motif was invented by proto-orthodox Christians to discredit the apocryphal Gospel of Thomas, a favorite of various non-orthodox Christians, such as the Gnostics and some Marcionites.

This Gospel of Thomas is a fascinating collection of rapid-fire quotes said to come straight from the mouth of Jesus. It takes no more than half an hour to read, start to finish, and it is well worth the time. You can Google and read it online for free.

The story seems to end with chapter twenty of John, which closes "Now Jesus did many other signs in the presence of the disciples, which are not written in this book; but these are written that you may believe that Jesus is the Christ, the Son of God, and that believing you may have life in his name."

Notice it is here that two completely different concepts are finally merged. The Christ, the Messiah, Yahweh's chosen one, the military leader in the mold of King David, whose role in freeing the Jewish people from servitude to Rome and restoring a society governed by Jewish Law had long been prophesied, has instead become the literal Son of God, for which there existed no Jewish prophecies, but in whom all people were now required to believe in order to have eternal life. This surely signaled the end of any hope for a continued relationship between Christianity and Judaism, a strictly monotheistic (one God only!) faith.

The gospel continues, however. Several of the disciples who were fishermen by trade were fishing one day when Jesus appeared anonymously on shore and hollered at them to switch their nets to the other side of their boat, and immediately they caught a huge haul of fish. As with his post-resurrection re-enactment of the Last Supper in Luke, this reprise of one of his greatest hits, when he nearly sank their boats with fish prior to calling them as his disciples, tipped them off that this again had to be the inexplicably hard-to-distinguish Jesus. After coming to shore, they stood right next to him at the little charcoal fire he had made to cook his fish, yet *still* they struggled to recognize him.

Whether or not Jesus was a shape-shifter before his death, it is pretty clear from these repeated episodes of his closest followers struggling to identify him that these biblical authors felt constrained to portray him as one after his death and resurrection. The apocryphal gospels take this possibility a fascinating step further.

Here is a final example, taken from the apocryphal Acts of John, Chapter 89: "And when we [John and James] left the place, wishing to follow him again, he again appeared to me, bald-headed but with a thick flowing beard; but to James he appeared as a youth whose beard was just starting."

Chapters ninety-four through ninety-six of Acts of John contain a spell-binding account of Jesus leading the disciples in a call-and-response dance circle. You can Google and read it online for free, too.

The Gospel of John closes with Jesus embarrassing Peter for infamously disowning him three times on the night of his crucifixion, followed by a confusing aside concerning the "disciple whom Jesus loved, who had lain close to his breast at the [Last] supper." Apparently a rumor had circulated in early Christian circles that this beloved disciple would survive until Jesus's triumphal return, and John (the gospel) tries to lay to rest this misconception. The author of John then seems to finger this beloved disciple as the source of the gospel's material, and adds the somewhat laughable pre-Digital Age proclamation that "there are also many other things which Jesus did; were every one of them to be written, I suppose that the world itself could not contain the books that would be written."

Of all the silly speculation concerning the "beloved disciple," perhaps the silliest is that he was Jesus's literal lover. There is better (but still unconvincing) evidence that Mary Magdalene served in that role. She is described as exactly that, Jesus's "lover," in the third century apocryphal Gospel of Philip, at verse 32. Whether that connotes a sexual relationship, an unconsummated romantic interest, or an extremely close friendship is hard to say. But bear in mind the moral climate of first century Palestine and the common knowledge of Jewish lore, including the story of sexual deviancy in Sodom and Gomorrah and Yahweh's wrath, not to mention Jesus's by-the-book responses to questions about the propriety of divorce. Given all of that, it seems very unlikely that Jesus and Mary Magdalene were an item.

The most moving exploration of this eternal mystery is doubtless found in the song "I Don't Know How to Love Him," sung by Mary Magdalene's character in the rock opera Jesus Christ Superstar, that glorious gift to the human race from Tim Rice and Andrew Lloyd Webber.

While it is beyond this book's ambitions to write an exhaustive history of two thousand years of Christianity, a brief summary of the adventures of Jesus's disciples in the aftermath of his crucifixion will help to complete the story of his life. In the New Testament book known as Acts of the Apostles, which follows the four gospels in the Bible and is the companion book to the Gospel of Luke, as mentioned earlier, Jesus reportedly spent forty days (there's that number again) after his crucifixion and resurrection appearing to his followers. After that time, he was reportedly carried up into heaven on a cloud, but not before telling his followers to expect a spiritual gift of the Holy Spirit from above. After choosing a new apostle and restoring their number to the preferred twelve, they waited.

This vital process of restoring their number to twelve sounds a bit like a superhero group such as the Avengers or the Guardians of the Galaxy replacing a fallen member.

In fairness, though, even mathematicians consider the number twelve to have a variety of remarkable properties. For example, under what is known in mathematics as number theory, twelve is one of only two "sublime" numbers, the other being 608655567 023837898967037173424316962265783077335188597O 52832486O51279169126⁴, which would be a very impractical number of apostles.

According to Acts of the Apostles, the gift arrived on the day known as Pentecost, which was a Jewish celebration of the day Moses had supposedly received the Ten Commandments from Yahweh on Mount Sinai. Jesus's followers, said to number at the time a mere one hundred and twenty, were all together when "suddenly a sound came from heaven like the rush of a mighty wind," understood to be the Holy Spirit. Acts describes them as having "tongues as of fire…resting on each one of them" as they were filled with this spirit and spontaneously began speaking in a variety of languages (Acts 2:1-4).

They then preached to the multilingual crowds in Jerusalem, articulating the strange new message that, not only was Jesus resurrected from the dead, he was a different kind of Messiah. No, he wasn't the long-awaited one who would drive out the Romans, but rather one who had the power to forgive the sins of those who repented, were baptized, and believed in him. Then they too would be filled with this divine, spiritual wind.

Well, the show they put on that day must have been impressive, because it reportedly won three thousand new converts on the spot, and right there the Christian Church was born, with an inaugural membership, it seems, of 3,120.

In one of several clear examples in Acts of communal living by the earliest Christians, these new converts then "sold their possessions and goods and distributed them to all, as any had need" (Acts 2:44–45). But for some reason, these examples bounce right off modern Christians, causing them not even a twitch of cognitive dissonance. As we will see in subsequent parts of this book, the selective application of biblical principles must always take place exclusively on their terms.

According to Acts the twelve apostles, led by Peter and John, continued to preach this gospel of a new kind of Christ all around Jerusalem. They repeatedly angered Jewish leaders and amazed crowds with their eloquence and miraculous healing powers. The book of Acts says that after receiving a beating on the orders of a Temple council, they then "left the presence of the council, rejoicing that they were counted worthy to suffer dishonor for the name [of Jesus]" (Acts 5:41).

Little did those early Christians know they were laying the groundwork for a dubious tradition as revered as any in Christianity, one unaffected by the virtual takeover by Christians of control over most of the planet: imagining that one is being persecuted or even martyred for one's Christian faith.

A figure appears in chapter six of Acts whose life—or more accurately, whose *death*—played an important role in the history of Christianity. This man, an early Christian with "the face of an angel" and the now familiar name of Stephen, was accused by jealous, disgruntled locals of blasphemy and brought before a Temple council. What followed was apparently some of the greatest (and longest) impromptu speechmaking ever witnessed.

Chapter seven of Acts recounts how Stephen gave a tough-talking lecture to Temple officials in which he recounted in minute detail the entire history of the Jewish people from memory and made the case for the crucified and resurrected Jesus being the long-awaited Christ of Jewish prophecy, which caused the officials to "grind their teeth against him" in anger. Stephen then went an important step further, declaring, "Behold, I see the heavens opened, and the Son of man standing at the right hand of God." That is, he apparently saw Jesus as some form of deity alongside Yahweh in heaven. Well, this was too much. The officials "cried out with a loud voice and stopped their ears and rushed together upon him. Then they cast him out of the city" so the crowd could pelt him to death with stones as punishment for his blasphemy.

One can only imagine that nothing perked up a dreary day back then like a public stoning done with the official blessing of Temple leaders.

Stephen's speech became rather important in the history of Church literature and the development of modern Christology (again, the branch of Christian theology relating to the person, nature, and role of Jesus). In addition to harshly condemning the Jews for not accepting Jesus as the Messiah, Stephen helped pave the way to the Christian understanding of Jesus as a literal deity that the religion now takes for granted. This radical concept, mentioned earlier in the context of the Gospel of John (written *after* Acts), was brand new at the time of Stephen's death and nowhere to be found in writing. Who would articulate it on paper (or papyrus) for generations of Christians to come? The answer was lurking at the outer edge of that angry crowd stoning Stephen to death outside of Jerusalem.

If you are keeping score, we have now gone from the belief of a tribe of herdsmen—the Jewish people—that a human Messiah would arrive and lead them to military victory over Rome to a failed human Messiah to a supernatural resurrected Messiah with a role unknown to Jewish prophecy to the literal Son of God and co-equal of Yahweh reaching out to the whole world.

While the crowd pushed and shoved to get close enough to throw their best stones, the ones they'd been saving for just such an occasion, at poor Stephen, he of the angelic face and sharp tongue, a lowlife opportunist had already set up shop farther back. According to Acts, this man, Saul of Tarsus, was taking payments from the crowd to run a literal coat-check at Stephen's stoning. Because really, is there anything more frustrating than wasting a great stoning rock with a bad throw because of a bulky cloak?

After watching Stephen's stoning death with approval, Saul, an agent of the Jewish establishment, took off for Damascus (in modern Syria) armed with formal letters that made him a literal bounty hunter of Christians, whom he obviously hated. However, according to chapter nine of Acts, as he neared Damascus flashing lights surrounded him. He fell to the ground, struck suddenly blind, and heard the voice of Jesus say, "Saul, Saul, why do you persecute me?" This voice instructed him to go to the city and meet a certain man named Anani'as. Meanwhile, Jesus separately appeared to Anani'as and told him to meet Saul, whose reputation as an enemy of Christians he'd already heard about. Jesus reassured him, "Go, for he is a chosen instrument of mine *to carry my name before the Gentiles* and kings and the sons of Israel" (emphasis added).

And so it began. Acts states that Anani'as met with Saul (whose Roman name was Paul), cured his temporary blindness, and baptized him. Saul, with new vision in both literal and figurative senses, began preaching the gospel immediately to whoever would listen, declaring that Jesus "is the Son of God." And there you have it: a Christology portraying Jesus as a literal deity, the Son of God, combined with an openness to the conversion of Gentiles, all wrapped up in the person of Saul/Paul, a passionate, tireless evangelist and gifted writer. And the rest, as they say, is history—two thousand years of it. Today there are about two billion Christians in the world and maybe fourteen million Jews. That's a ratio of 143 to 1. So you can plainly see what a fateful moment this was for a tiny cult of Jewish heretics.

Saul/Paul claimed he frequently had lengthy supernatural conversations with Jesus, most of them at night.

There were other things pointing early Christians toward welcoming various Gentile groups to the nascent faith (to them the term Gentile included both non-Jews and non-practicing Jews). For one thing they needed to grow the movement. For another they no doubt sought political cover, so to speak. They surely needed more friends in high places for their own protection since they, unlike modern Western Christians, were frequently the targets of actual persecution, not mere incidental slights. And there were additional signs, such as the dream Peter had in a trance, where he was shown many different kinds of animals and a voice told him, contrary to Jewish Law, to eat whichever ones he wished. This, he decided, was God telling him "that I should not call any man common or unclean."

By our modern hygienic standards, probably ALL of the people from that era would be considered unclean!

The subsequent life and times of Saint Paul could fill an entire book by itself, as it featured shipwrecks, arrests, beatings, his own stoning (which he survived), imprisonments, harrowing escapes, natural disasters, poverty, and hunger. However, the most important features of it are:

1. Paul traveled endlessly, successfully spreading his message and starting churches all around the Mediterranean during a critical early stage in the growth of the Christian Church.

2. One of the rare early Christians with a formal education, Paul wrote brilliantly about his faith in letters to congregations he'd started in various cities in and around the Mediterranean. These letters were widely copied and shared and became the earliest sacred writings of the church, older than all four of the gospels. (Note: serious biblical historians *all* agree today that some of the letters attributed to Paul were actually written by other authors pseudonymously.)

3. In his letters Paul was the first person in known history to develop Christian principles of theology, such as his clear view of Jesus as the savior of mankind, preordained to die for the remission (washing away) of human sin; and his concept that salvation is based strictly on faith and not "works of the law." The latter concept would heavily influence Martin Luther fifteen hundred years later and loom large in the Protestant Reformation of the Catholic Church.

4. Despite intense resistance from church leaders in Jerusalem, Paul argued passionately for the inclusion of non-Jews in the new church and a movement away from Jewish Law and tradition.

Anyone who has heard the well-known "faith, hope, and love" passage from First Corinthians read at a wedding can appreciate the poetic flair on display in Paul's writing.

Ultimately Paul was arrested a final time in Jerusalem in 57 A.D. and charged with heresy. He exercised his right as a Roman citizen to appeal directly to Caesar, and after two years of incarceration and one last shipwreck, he arrived in Rome, where he spent his final days under house arrest before dying. Some think he was martyred, which he would have no doubt preferred to any less dramatic exit.

In one of the most delightful of his many colorful lessons, Paul counseled the faithful at the church in Rome that "if your enemy is hungry, feed him; if he is thirsty, give him drink; for by so doing you will heap burning coals upon his head. Do not be overcome by evil, but overcome evil with good" (Romans 12:20).

So there you have it. A Jewish boy named Jesus was born in the Middle East two thousand years ago, some say in Bethlehem but more likely in Nazareth, where he grew up. As a young man, he went off to the wilderness, met an ascetic named John the Baptist, and underwent a spiritual transformation. When he came back, he spent perhaps a few years teaching and supposedly performing miraculous deeds in Galilee for a fairly motley group of followers. His charismatic speeches had a number of themes but none more common than his relentless criticisms of immodesty, remorselessness, greed, false piety, hypocrisy, and church corruption. Eventually he went to Jerusalem and started a riot in the Jewish Temple, raging at concessionaires. He was arrested, tried, beaten, and executed by Roman crucifixion. Many of his followers claimed they saw him alive afterward, and a religion was born—one bearing little resemblance to Jesus's own Jewish faith. This transition from Judaism to Christianity was accomplished largely through the passionate writings of a Jew named Saul of Tarsus, better known to Christians as Saint Paul. That's the whole story.

Although it's plain from the letters of Paul that the winds of change were already blowing before the four written gospels surfaced, no one can say exactly when Christianity separated itself from Judaism once and for all. It did take a while. On the front end, we know that during Paul's final visit to Jerusalem in 57 A.D., early Christian leaders there still felt so beholden to Jewish Law that they forced him to undergo a humiliating Jewish purification ritual. On the back end, it's known from surviving records that in 98 A.D., under the Roman emperor Nerva, Christians were finally exempted from the annual tax paid by the Jews to Rome, the *fiscus Judaicus*. So sometime between 57 A.D. when this cleansing took place to get the Gentile off of Paul, so to speak, and 98 A.D., when this "Jew tax" was excused, the important transition from a Jewish heresy to a brand new religion took place.

Never known for a lack of nerve, Paul boldly strolled into the Temple in Jerusalem after this cleansing and was nearly torn to pieces by the crowd. He had to turn himself in to Roman guards for fear of what Jewish authorities would do to him.

Yet it would be misleading to suggest that official Church Christology settled quickly into a focused picture based solely on Paul's letters and the Gospel of John. Because even after Orthodox Judaism had been left far behind, Christian theology continued to thrash around wildly for centuries, with many competing views jockeying for position, some of which would today be considered downright scandalous or even bizarre.

On one end were the **Ebionites**, converted Jews who maintained Jewish customs and believed Jesus was in fact the human Messiah chosen to save the world, but certainly not the divine Son of God. On the other end were the **Marcionites**, who believed the vengeful Jewish god Yahweh might have created the world, but a different, rival god sent Jesus, who only appeared human, to save the world from the wrath of Yahweh. In between were a wide variety of slightly different formulas. There were also a number of different **Gnostic** groups, who believed Jesus was a divine cosmic messenger of sorts, who came into our world to leave coded instructions for the salvation of special individuals who had a divine spark in them.

But all of that changed forever with perhaps the single most important development in early, post-Paul Christian history: the conversion of Roman Emperor Constantine the Great, who reigned from 306 to 337 A.D. In 313 he issued the Edict of Milan, which formally legalized Christian worship.

Constantine's reasons for converting to Christianity are not well understood, but popular lore says that in 312, at the Battle of Milvian Bridge (which spans the Tiber River near Rome), while preparing to do battle for control of the Western Roman Empire against his rival, Maxentius, he spotted a cross-shaped light in the sky and the words *"En touto nika"* ("In this sign conquer"). He converted, the legend goes, out of gratitude for his subsequent victory.

It is interesting to observe that this god of *Hebrew* origin, who spoke *Aramaic* while on Earth, wrote to Constantine, a Roman *(Latin)* soldier using *Greek* letters in the sky.

This episode laid the groundwork for two revolting Christian traditions: waging war in the name of Jesus, and giving thanks and credit to him after triumph on the field of battle.

This latter custom finds only slightly less appalling expression in the modern practice of athletes who, forgetting Jesus's clear statement that God "makes his sun rise on the evil and the good," credit him for victory on the playing field.

The next pivotal thing Constantine did was to convene the 325 A.D. meeting of nearly two thousand church leaders in the city of Nicea, in what is now Turkey, with instructions not to leave without producing an official statement of Christian beliefs, one that eliminated all disagreement on the subject and that the church would permanently adopt. The one they came up with—which included the Nicene Creed well known to the many millions of young Christians forced to memorize it—is the one the church still uses to this day. Jesus was both the Son of God and God. God the Father was God. Last but not least, the Holy Spirit was God. They were all part of a triune God concept that was already popular despite scant support for it in sacred writings. It is now widely accepted by the world's Christians.

Pope Sylvester, who served from 314 to 335 A.D., supposedly had a dream about the conversion of Constantine which he interpreted to mean "now is poison poured into the church."

The Bible itself was still surprisingly unsettled at the time of this Council of Nicea. The oldest surviving reference to the twenty-seven books we now know as the New Testament is a 367 A.D. letter to Egyptian churches from Bishop Athanasius of Alexandria (Egypt) about which books could be read as authentic scripture during worship. An official collection of the sixty-six books of today's Bible wouldn't emerge until sometime around 390 to 400 A.D., selected and arranged over the course of several church councils held at the city of Hippo Regius in what is now Algeria in North Africa. This was the home of the famous theologian/philosopher St. Augustine of Hippo, author of the well-known book *Confessions*. North Africa at that time was a stronghold of Christian belief.

Though it is mind-boggling to contemplate, Confessions is widely thought to be the first example in Western literature of a book in which the author dared show the audacity to write about...himself.

With the military might of Rome backing it and an agreed-upon the-ology and Bible in hand, the Catholic Church went on to dominate the next one thousand-plus years of Western history. This took place notwith-standing some pretty big hiccups, such as the fall of the Roman Empire; the rise and spread of Islam through much of the Middle East, Asia, and Africa beginning in the late seventh century; and the so-called Great Schism of the eleventh century, when long-simmering conflicts between church authorities in Rome and Constantinople (now Istanbul, Turkey) led to a massive East-West split that left two official Christian Churches where there had been one: the Roman Catholic Church (still the world's largest) and the Eastern Orthodox Church (still number two).

The theological sticking points between the two Churches would seem almost trivial to a non-Christian. In fact, to an outside observer, their differences would appear to lie mainly in the areas of geography, architectural design, and official clothing.

EASTERN ORTHODOX
MAJORITY OR SIGNIFICANT
MINORITY RELIGION.

The next really cataclysmic development within Christianity, the period of the so-called Protestant Reformation, took place during the sixteenth century. Please bear in mind that there was a great deal of activity within the Church during the lengthy period I am fast-forwarding past. On the bright side, some glorious cathedrals were built, many of which are still standing today. However, it was a predominantly gloomy period for Christianity full of disease, death, and rampant stupidity, so for now I will merely summarize it with reference to some of its recurring themes:

- Shameful sexual misconduct

- Blatant nepotism

- Corrupting entanglement with government

- Knifepoint conversions

- Ethnic cleansing

- Trafficking in phony relics

- War after war fought in the name of God

- *Non-adherence to fundamental church doctrines*

(Numerous hair-raising examples of these Church scandals can be found in part five of this book.)

Believe it or not, with the exception of some whispering about sexual peccadilloes, well-cowed Christians over the years were mostly OK with the items on that list—except for that last one. And so, like Jesus before them, a series of influential figures began loudly criticizing the Church for its hypocrisy. Around the turn of the fifteenth century, first John Wycliffe at Oxford University (in England) and then Jan Huss in Prague (in what is now the Czech Republic) began speaking and writing openly about church abuses. In no mood to fool around, the Vatican in Rome declared Hus a heretic and ordered him burned at the stake in 1415. Not fully satisfied, in 1428 it dug up the body of Wycliffe, who had died in 1384, but whose writings had inspired Hus, and put the torch to his corpse also. These were, shall we say, interesting times in the Church.

One hundred years later, a colorful German figure with the now familiar name Martin Luther splashed onto the scene in Europe. Luther was an Augustinian monk and later a priest and professor of theology who was influenced by Wycliffe, Hus, and other critics of the Vatican. He had a wide variety of complaints, but the main one was his fiery opposition to the then-common Church practice of selling "indulgences" for the forgiveness of sin. Yes, the Catholic Church was offering salvation for sale. On October 31, 1517, Luther nailed his critical Ninety-Five Theses to the door of the church at Wittenberg University in Germany, and the so-called Protestant Reformation was born.

Luther originally pledged to be a monk in exchange for God's saving his life during a thunderstorm. This resulted in a lifetime of turmoil and ridicule, but spared him the misery of having to complete his training to become a lawyer.

In response to his relentless criticisms of the Church, Vatican officials in 1521 dragged Luther before a formal inquisition, well-known to many generations of Lutheran Sunday school children for its delightful name, the Diet of Worms (a city in Germany). He refused to recant his theses at the Diet and was officially declared a heretic and excommunicated. Luther went into hiding and was declared an outlaw. It became a criminal offense to give him food or shelter. Anyone was permitted to kill him on sight without legal consequence. No, the Church did not play games in those days.

During a period spent in hiding at Wartburg Castle in Eisenach, Germany, Luther reportedly slipped into town from time to time concealed under a literal suit of armor to drink beer in local pubs.

Luther's accomplishments, though extraordinary, were utterly condemned by Church authorities in Rome. As a brief sampling of his work, Luther:

1. Translated the entire Bible into German, based on his belief that common Church members had the right to access the material and make their own religious observations without Church interference.

2. Turned around the idea of being saved by pious religious displays. He vehemently opposed the idea that you could earn God's gifts and went so far as to claim that every good work contrived to attract God's favor was a literal sin. *Read that last sentence again.*

3. Opposed the mandatory celibacy of priesthood. After his excommunication, he helped twelve nuns escape from a Cistercian convent by hiding them in herring barrels, and then married one of them, Katharina von Bora.

4. Adamantly denied the concept of papal infallibility—the idea that the pope in Rome was incapable of error and reflected the literal will of God on Earth.

Luther was a typical beer-and-sausage German, and claimed he had at times warded off Satan with his own intestinal gases.

To make a long story short, Luther became the most prominent of a number of Protestant reformers who wrote and lectured extensively in opposition to the gross corruption that was running riot within the Roman Church at that time (others included Huldrych Zwingli and John Calvin in Switzerland). The distribution of their writings was no doubt helped by the invention of the printing press in that very same part of the world in that very same era. These were fateful times.

Their reform movements led ultimately to the establishment of a variety of new splinter-group Churches, which were the precursors to many of the Protestant denominations that make up around 20 to 25 percent of the Christian presence in the world today.

Adding to the confusion, it was around this same time in England that King Henry VIII resolved a dispute with the Vatican over the annulment of his marriage by petulantly establishing the rival Church of England and placing himself in charge of it. As a result, we also have what is known as the Anglican Church, which has a current membership of more than 85 million people.

This was not strictly an intellectual revolution. Many people died in conflicts over theology, and the century that followed was among the bloodiest in European history.

Part three of this book contains summaries of the differences between these various Christian Churches.

As you might have guessed already, the Church in Rome was unmoved by these assorted protests, and though it was shamed into halting the sale of indulgences, it changed little else in direct response to the bloody upheaval. In the end the principal effect of the Protestant Reformation on the Catholic Church was, in a manner of speaking, a significant loss of market share. That's it. Which brings us to our current situation: the largely Christian world we live in, with two out of every seven human beings claiming to believe that Jesus Christ is God, and more than half of them still loyal to the Roman Catholic Church.

Congratulations! You now know more than probably ninety percent of those Christians about their own faith, but what you do with that knowledge is up to you. If you'd like to use it to fight back against tiresome Fundamentalist intrusions in your life, keep on reading.

PART TWO

KNOW THE FIVE BIBLICAL FALLACIES

Let's say a cadre of Christian soldiers has you cornered. The fighting is furious, and every logical argument you swing at them seems to bounce off their dense exterior. Wouldn't it help to know where the cracks in their armor are located?

Well, you are in luck my friend. Because fortunately, many popular elements of common Christian belief are, it has to be said, just plain demonstrably *wrong*. Either they are totally contradicted within the pages of the Christian Bible itself, or they are wholly unsupported or even disproved by outside research. Some of them are damnably important, and I am here to tell you all about them.

The following five time-honored Christian concepts—let's call them **The Five Fallacies©**—are all of them vital aspects of Christian belief, yet they are either so clearly false or utterly dubious that you should probably memorize them, at least by name. Why? Because exposing these Five Fallacies© can be a real game-changer when you find yourself face to face with an aggressive Fundamentalist, that's why. Just whip out your copy of this handy book for the details and you'll have that break- room preacher back-pedaling and on the ropes in no time. Hint: it helps to own several copies and keep them stashed in those places—at work, in the car, in the foyer—where you can get to them fast when you're most likely to need them.

The First Fallacy: The Inerrancy of the Bible

Where, really, do we start with this issue? The fact is there are enough undeniable historical errors, geographical errors, biological errors, transcription errors, and internal contradictions in the Bible to fill many volumes. We already touched upon some of them in part one of this book. What follows is a partial list of the reasons that even renowned Christian apologist C.S. Lewis, author of beloved Christian books such as *The Chronicles of Narnia* and the man who was fondly known as "the apostle to the skeptics," ultimately threw his arms up after years of painstaking research and admitted there was no rational case for a flawless Christian Bible. Here you will find a few really big problems for advocates of Biblical inerrancy followed by a list of smaller ones. Together they ought to be enough to ward off marauding gangs of unsavory Fundamentalists every time.

Two Conflicting Creation Stories

The problems start early in the Bible, in the first book of the Old Testament. Creationists who base their beliefs on the Bible will need to explain which one of the two conflicting creation stories appearing in Genesis they find so obviously superior to Darwin's theory of evolution: the first one at Genesis 1:1-2:3* or the one that follows at Genesis 2:4-25.

*It is startling how similar this first creation story actually is to conventional scientific explanations of the origins of the universe and life on Earth when adjusted for the single element of time. Both posit the same basic sequence: 1) a sudden expansion of energy, 2) a foundational role played by the presence of water, 3) the establishment of our solar system, 4) the separation of land and water on Earth, 5) the emergence of marine life, 6) the emergence of land animals, and 7) the emergence of *Homo sapiens*, all in roughly that order. Christian Fundamentalists, unsurprisingly, are too dim-witted and stubborn to notice and take credit for this.

Some Christians will tell you they aren't so different. Oh, really? Here is the first creation story, slightly abridged:

1. First day: In the beginning God created the heaven and the earth. God said "Let there be light," and there was light, and the evening and the morning were the first day.

2. Second day: God separated the "firmament" or heavens from the waters.

3. Third day: God separated the waters from dry land, and placed seed-bearing plants and trees on the land.

4. Fourth day: God placed the sun, moon, and stars in the sky to rule over the day and over the night, "for signs, and for seasons, and for days, and years" (unclear how the prior three days were measured).

5. Fifth day: God created "the great sea monsters" and every other creature that flies or swims.

6. Sixth day: God created "cattle, and creeping things, and beast of the earth after his kind," and followed that up by creating man, "in the image of God created he him; male and female created he them."

7. Seventh day: God rested.

Contrast this with the second creation story that appears immediately after it, at Genesis 2:4:

1. "In the day that the Lord God made the earth and the heavens," before vegetation, rain, or mankind, "a mist went up from the earth and watered the whole face of the ground."

2. "Then the Lord God formed man [not woman] of dust from the ground, and breathed into his nostrils the breath of life; and man became a living being."

3. "The Lord God planted a garden in Eden, in the east; and there he put the man whom he had formed."

4. God put trees in the garden, including the notorious tree of knowledge of good and evil.

5. God told man the tree was off-limits.

6. God created the birds and all land animals, and man gave each a name.

7. God caused man to fall into a deep sleep, swiped one of his ribs, and used it to create woman.

You probably already know the rest of this alternative version. The serpent, described as "more subtle than any other wild creature," tempted woman with the fruit of the notorious tree; she ate it, then gave it to man, who also ate it. God found them out, man blamed woman, woman blamed serpent, and God expelled them both from Eden.

So is this really a second creation story? Absolutely. God rearranged the heavens, Earth, and water, then created man, then plants, then animals, then woman (from man). The most serious of the clashes between the two stories is that in the first, Adam and Eve were created *simultaneously, after* the plants and other animals, and in the second Adam was God's *first* creation following the "misting" of the Earth, followed by plants, then animals, *then* woman, *from* man. No explanation is given for these obvious discrepancies. But let me guess, contentious Christian: you're about to create one. While you're at it, why don't you create two completely different explanations and then claim they don't conflict?

Two Conflicting Sets of the Ten Commandments.

Unfortunately for Christians claiming the Bible is infallible, there are likewise conflicting versions of the famed Ten Commandments—a total of three sets if you want to get technical about it. The first of two twin sets appears in the Old Testament book of Exodus in chapter twenty, and a second, nearly identical set appears in the book of Deuteronomy in chapter five. Here is the substance of those first two similar sets combined:

I. You shall not have other gods before Yahweh.

II. You shall not make "graven images" or likenesses or worship them.

III. You shall not take the name of God in vain.

IV. Remember the Sabbath Day (the last day of the week) and keep it holy—meaning no work.

V. Honor your father and your mother if you want to live a long, good life.

VI. You shall not kill.

VII. You shall not commit adultery.

VIII. You shall not steal.

IX. You shall not bear false witness against your neighbor.

X. You shall not covet your neighbor's house, wife, servants, animals, or anything else that belongs to your neighbor.

To be fair, the commandments in Exodus 20 and Deuteronomy 5 really are almost interchangeable. But it's an important list, the Bible claims that God gave it directly to Moses. Variations of any kind probably shouldn't be found in such matters. So in equal fairness I should note that there are several very small differences.

I will also point out the exceedingly obvious fact that millions of Christians routinely violate a number of these classic Ten Commandments with hardly a thought every week. The second (images), third (swearing), fourth (Sabbath), and tenth (coveting) in particular come to mind. That being the case, you should probably make a point of asking the pious Fundamentalist standing before you if he strictly observes the Sabbath, and by that I mean no work of any kind—no grocery shopping, watering the plants, doing laundry, or making lunch. Therefore a Christian claiming to observe the Sabbath "in his own way" might as well be claiming he observes the commandments against stealing or even killing in his own way. You'll want to remind him that lying about it would be a violation of a separate commandment.

While you're at it, you might also ask if his home contains "any likeness of anything that is in heaven above, or that is in the earth beneath, or that is in the water under the earth." Because that, too, violates these Ten Commandments (i.e. the second).

One could certainly assume that the bobble-head doll of a revered sports figure sitting on a shelf in a child's room, surrounded by matching bubblegum cards, posters, and memorabilia, would easily violate the Second Commandment, and there are countless other possible examples. Catholics have recast the language of this commandment (pardon the pun) to appease their voracious appetite for iconic imagery.

The real problem for self-righteous Christians appears not in the minor discrepancies regarding these two twin versions of the classic ten, however, but in the much lesser-known *third* set of commandments, found in Exodus chapter thirty-four. Because for one thing, it is a downright bizarre list, to the point where you are tempted to think it is some kind of awful mistake. And for another, it plainly states that *it* is the true list of the Ten Commandments, which forces you to wonder if the version so well known to Sunday school children and federal courts of appeal is the aberration.

The problem began when Moses smashed the original stone tablets given to him by Yahweh on Mount Sinai, those thought to contain the classic ten listed above. He did so in a fit of rage after seeing his fellow Israelites worshipping an idol, a golden calf. A replacement set was needed, and the one given, for whatever reason, turned out like *this*, and I'm not kidding. Ladies and gentlemen, I give you God's Ten Commandments!

I. You shall worship no other god, for the Lord, whose name is Jealous, is a jealous god.

II. You shall make for yourself no molten gods.

III. The feast of unleavened bread you shall keep, and so on.

IV. All that opens the womb is mine, all your male cattle, the firstlings of cow and sheep, and so forth.

V. Six days shall you work, but on the seventh day you shall rest; in plowing time and in harvest you shall rest.

VI. You shall observe the feast of weeks, the first fruits of wheat harvest, and the feast of ingathering at the year's end.

VII. Three times a year shall all your males appear before the Lord God, the God of Israel, et cetera.

VIII. You shall not offer the blood of my sacrifice with leaven; neither shall the sacrifice of the feast of Passover be left until the morning.

IX. The first of the first fruits of your ground you shall bring to the house of the Lord your God.

X. You shall not boil a kid (baby goat) in its mother's milk.

Now, I know what you're probably thinking—*"What kind of monster boils a kid in its mother's milk?"* No, the other thing you're probably thinking—*"Oh, right. Where in the hell did that crazy list of commandments come from?"* That's better. And the answer is clearly stated in Exodus 34:1, where Yahweh (or Jealous, as he is apparently also known) told Moses, "Cut two tables of stone like the first; and I will write upon the tables the words that were on the first tables, which you broke." In other words, Yahweh authenticates *these ten* (see Exodus 34:14-28).

So this is a big problem for Christianity, and it is pretty obvious that either A) there are multiple, conflicting sets of the Ten Commandments that have next to nothing in common other than prohibitions against other gods, graven images, and work on the Sabbath; or B) someone made a mistake. So you tell me, infuriating Christian. And shame on you if you've been boiling kids in their mother's milk.

Jesus had little to say about the Ten Commandments in the four gospels. When asked in Matthew 22 which is the greatest commandment in the law, he seemed to disregard the better-known ten, responding, "You shall love the Lord with all your heart, and with all your soul, and with all your mind. This is the great and first commandment. And a second is like it, You shall love your neighbor as yourself. On these two commandments depend all the law and the prophets." Well said, Jesus.

While we are on the subject of the Ten Commandments, I might as well add that even though the Koran, the Bible of the Muslim faith, contains no numeric list of commandments, it does, in various places, echo every single one of the traditional Jewish/Christian commandments except the observance of the Sabbath, which might as well be omitted from the Christian list as well.

Here we go again.

The Dubious Lineage of Jesus.

Let's move on to the New Testament of the Christian Bible and the problem of Jesus's questionable family tree. As noted with disgust in various other sections of this book, the Hebrew preoccupation with male inheritance was so extreme that a man was expected to pound away sexually at his brother's grieving widow for as long as it took to impregnate her with a male heir. Jesus implicitly endorsed this ghastly practice at Matthew 22:23-33. So it's plain to see that under Jewish Law, in matters of genealogy, the woman played a perfunctory role hardly worthy of mention, while the male role was paramount. Keep this in mind as we examine the logical problems with Jesus's biblical lineage.

As mentioned earlier, the Bible has only two accounts of Jesus's birth, in the Gospels of Matthew and Luke. Both provide elaborate genealogies for him, and fittingly they do not even remotely begin to agree with one another. The account in Matthew purports to identify forty-one generations going back to Abraham through, of course, the beloved King David, the iconic figure representing the glorious period of Jewish self-rule. Most historians consider the period from Abraham to Jesus to cover roughly two thousand years, so bridging that gap in forty-one generations would require the average impregnation to be accomplished by a fiftyish-year-old father. For such a rugged period of history, fifty years sounds more like a generous estimate of life expectancy than an average age for fatherhood, so you can judge for yourself the reliability of Matthew's genealogy.

Not to be outdone, Luke traces Jesus's line back to Adam. Yes, *that* Adam. While Matthew settles for forty-one generations, Luke identifies seventy-seven, but they include less than half of the specific fathers named in Matthew. In fact the two lists have only two brief periods of agreement: one following Abraham and another preceding David. Luke does not even include the venerated King Solomon in his list, and the two don't even agree about something as basic and (for them) recent as the identity of Jesus's grandfather. And if the fifty-year-old fathers of

Matthew gave you pause, consider that if you accept the roughly 100,000-year estimate scientists typically give for the current lifespan of *Homo sapiens* as a species (stated conservatively), the seventy-seven generations of Luke must have lasted an average of almost 1,300 years each.

So the biblical accounts of the lineage of Jesus have serious problems, to say the very least, with both the grossly conflicting names of Jesus's ancestors, as well as with the apparent ages of the men they name.

But believe it or not, we still haven't gotten to the really bad part. Both of these purported genealogies contain a far more serious error: they trace the genealogy of Jesus through iconic heroes of Jewish history, such as Abraham, Isaac, Jacob, Jesse, and David, all the way to...*Joseph.* That's right, they lead to Jesus's adoptive stepfather. So the claim that Jesus fulfilled the ancient Jewish prophecy of a Messiah born from the House of David is based on an absolute howler of an oversight. The Jews of that era were so obsessed with patrilineal succession that the authors of Matthew and Luke apparently failed to even notice (much less mitigate) this staggering logical blunder. But we regret to inform you, aggravating Fundamentalist, we did notice. Now go away.

Historians also point out that surviving Roman records do not support the idea that Joseph was required to return to Bethlehem for a census. There was a census in 6 A.D. in the nearby areas of Judea, Samaria, and Idumea, but there was none in Galilee, the supposed home of Jesus's parents, and there is no evidence that a birth-city census of the kind described in Luke ever took place in any region under Roman imperial rule. Roman tax records, many of which survive, show that property was typically assessed at the subject's place of residence.

Jesus was likely born in Nazareth, but the Christmas card industry is eternally grateful for this biblical embellishment of his birth.

OK, so the creation story, the Ten Commandments, and the birth of Jesus are all messed up in the Bible. *Wow!* Those are some pretty important scenes from the Christian narrative to bear such obvious scars. And while they would be bad enough on their own, there are many, many more mix-ups, and some are extremely significant. So when you get cornered by nettlesome Fundamentalists claiming their inerrant Bible has all the answers for people today, just pull out this book and ask them these questions about the Old Testament:

- How many pairs of clean animals did Noah take onto his ark, one (Genesis 6:19) or seven (Genesis. 7:2)?

- How many days did the great flood last, forty (Genesis 7:17) or one hundred and fifty (Genesis 7:24)?

- How many tribes of Israel were there, and what were their names? The Old Testament initially names twelve—Reuben, Simeon, Levi, Judah, Issachar, Zebulun, Gad, Asher, Joseph, Benjamin, Dan, and Naphtali (Genesis 46:8-27)—but at other times seems to describe eleven or thirteen, and there is a degree of variation in the names included. In addition to the above twelve, the tribes which appear to receive mention include Menasseh, Ephraim, Machir, Gilead, Meroz, and Barak (See Judges 5:14-23, Numbers 10:14-27, 1 Chronicles 6:54-80).

- Was it an angel (Exodus 3:2) or was it Yahweh (Exodus 3:4) that appeared to Moses in the burning bush?

- Did Moses see Yahweh's face (Exodus 33:11) or didn't he (Exodus 33:18-20)?

- Did Moses receive the Ten Commandments on Mt. Sinai (Exodus 19:18) or Mt. Horeb (Deuteronomy 4:10-13)?

- Who constructed the Ark of the Covenant, Bezalel (Exodus 37:1) or Moses (Deuteronomy 10:1-3)?

- Was manna white with the taste of wafers made of honey (Exodus 16:31) or brown (the color of bdellium) with the taste of cakes baked with oil (Numbers 11:7-8)?

- Who really killed Goliath, David (1 Samuel 17:50) or Elhanan (2 Samuel 21:19)? (Note: translations vary with regard to this issue.)

- Did King Saul meet David before he killed the huge Philistine (1 Samuel 16:19-21) or after (1 Samuel 17:55-58)?

- What was the correct number of Philistine foreskins David paid King Saul for his daughter's hand in marriage (gross, I know), one hundred (2 Samuel 3:14) or two hundred (1 Samuel 18:27)?

- Who killed Saul? Was it an Amalekite (2 Samuel 1:5-10), the Philistines (2 Samuel 21:12), the Lord himself (1 Chronicles 10:13-14), or was it a suicide (1 Samuel 31:3-4)? And did his sons die with him (1 Chronicles 10:6) or not (2 Samuel 2:8)?

- Did Yahweh tell David not to build him a house because he, the Lord, had never had one before, and had always gone from tent to tent like Israel itself (1 Chronicles 17:4-5), or was it because David had been a warrior who had shed blood (1 Chronicles 28:3)?

- Did King Solomon have seven hundred wives and three hundred concubines (1 Kings 11:3) (Note: that is Wilt Chamberlain territory!) or sixty wives and eighty concubines (Song of Solomon 6:8)?

- Were the dimensions of Solomon's temple those described in 1 Kings 7:2-16 or the completely different ones from 2 Chronicles 3:3-15 and 2 Kings 25:17?

- Did King Nebuchadnezzar drag eighteen thousand Jewish captives to Babylon (2 Kings 24:14-16) or was it 4,600 (Jeremiah 52:28-30)?

And if those abrasive Fundamentalists claim they can't answer every little question about murky things buried deep in the dusty Old Testament, it's time to ask them these questions about the New Testament:

- Were Jesus and Mary from Bethlehem (Matthew 2:1) or Nazareth (Luke 1:26-27, Luke 2:4-5)?

- Did Joseph and Mary go to Jerusalem (Luke 2:22) or Egypt (Matthew 2:14-15) after Jesus's birth?

- Did Jesus begin his ministry before John was imprisoned (John 3:22-24) or after (Matthew 4:12-17)?

- Were disciples Simon and Andrew from Capernaum (Mark 1:21-29) or Beth-sa'ida (John 1:44)?

- What were the correct names of the so-called Twelve Apostles, and how many of them were there? The Synoptic Gospels of Matthew (chapter 10), Mark (chapter 3), and Luke (chapter 6) are in agreement about only Simon **Peter**, his brother **Andrew**, **James** the son of Zebedee, **John** the son of Zebedee, **Philip**, **Bartholomew**, **Thomas** Didymus, **Matthew** the publican, **James**

Alphaeus, and **Judas Iscariot**. That's ten. In places, Mark and Luke seem to add Levi Alphaeus the publican, but Christians expect us to understand that Matthew and Levi are one and the same person. Luke also lists Judas who is the son of James the son of Zebedee, whom we shall call **Judas (not Iscariot)**, and **Simon the Zealot**. Matthew and Mark add Labbaeus **Thaddeus** and **Simon the Canaanite**, who may or may not have also been known as Simon the Zealot. The Gospel of John names only eight: Simon Peter, James and John the sons of Zebedee, Philip, Thomas Didymus, Judas Iscariot, Judas (not Iscariot), and someone named **Nathanael of Cana**. John references a possible additional pair of apostles without naming them (John 21:2). Paul's letter to the Galatians clearly identifies **James the brother of Jesus** as one of the apostles (Galatians 1:19). Confused? So am I.

- Did Jesus want his disciples to preach to all nations (Matthew 28:18) or to the Jews only (Matthew 10:5-6)?

- Was Jairus's daughter dying (Mark 5:23, Luke 8:42) or dead (Matthew 9:18) when Jesus went to heal her?

- Did Jesus's disciples fast (Matthew 6:16) or not (Mark 2:18)?

- Did Jesus overturn the money tables in the Temple at the beginning of his ministry (John 2:13-15) or at the end (Mark 11:15)?

- Did the fig tree cursed by Jesus die immediately (Matthew 21:19) or overnight (Mark 11:13-20)?

- Should people undecided about Jesus be considered for him (Luke 9:50) or against him (Luke 11:23)?

- Did Jesus ride into Jerusalem on a colt (Mark 11:7, Luke 19:35), an ass (John 12:14), or, most improbably, both a colt *and* an ass simultaneously (Matthew 21:6-7)? (Note: by now it should not surprise you to learn that the ass-colt combination was meant to fulfill two contradictory Jewish prophecies.)

- Did the Last Supper occur on the day of the Passover meal (Matthew 26:19, Mark 14:12, Luke 22:7-13) or on the day before it (John 13:1-2, 18:28)?

- When asked at his trial if he was the Christ, did Jesus say "I am" (Mark 14:61-62), "You have said so" (Matthew 26:63-64), "If I tell you, you will not believe" (Luke 22:67), or "Why do you ask me? Ask those who have heard me, what I said to them; they know what I said" (John 18:21)?

- What color was Jesus's robe on the night of his crucifixion, scarlet (Matthew 27:27-28) or purple (John 19:2)?

- How many times did the rooster crow before Peter's denial of Jesus the night of his arrest, once (Matthew 26:74-75) or twice (Mark 14:71-72)?

- Did Judas Iscariot hang himself (Matthew 27:5) or did he fall and "burst asunder...and all his bowels gushed out" (Acts 1:18)?

- Who carried Jesus's cross, Jesus himself (John 19:17) or Simon the Cyrenian (Mark 15:21)?

- Was Jesus crucified on the day of the Passover meal (John 18:28) or the day after (Luke 22:13)?

- Was it the third hour of the day (Mark 15:25) or the sixth (John 19:14-18) when Jesus was crucified?

- Was Jesus mocked by both of the criminals crucified alongside him (Mark 15:32) or by just the one and defended and praised by the other (Luke 23: 39-41)?

- Did Jesus drink on the cross (John 19:30) or not (Mark 15:23)?

- Were the last words of Jesus on the cross "My God, my God, why hast thou forsaken me?" (Matthew 27:46, Mark 15:34); "Father, into thy hands I commend my spirit!" (Luke 23:46); or "It is finished!" (John 19:30)?

- Did Jesus's followers stand near him during his crucifixion (John 19:25-26) or at a distance (Matthew 27:55)?

- Did Jesus die before the temple curtain was torn in half (Mark 15:37-38) or after (Luke 23:45-46)? Biblical historians consider the point to be crucial.

- Did the centurion at the scene of Jesus's crucifixion describe him as an innocent man (Luke 23:47) or "the Son of God" (Mark 15:39)?

- Did Joseph of Arimathea ask for the body of Jesus courageously (Mark 15:43) or secretly (John 19:38)?

- How many women went to Jesus's tomb on Easter morning, one (John 20:1), two (Matthew 28:1), three (Mark 16:1), or more than three (Luke 24:10)?

- Was the tomb already open (Mark 16:4, Luke 24:2, John 20:1) or not (Matthew 28:2), guarded (Matthew 28:4) or not (Mark 16:2)?

- Did the women at the tomb see an angel (Matthew 28:2), a young man (Mark 16:5), two men (Luke 24:4), or two angels (John 20:11-12)?

- What did the women do after they left, run and tell the others (Matthew 28:8, Luke 24:9) or flee in fear and tell no one (Mark 16:8)?

- Did the resurrected Jesus first appear to his women followers at the tomb (John 20:15-16), near the tomb (Matthew 28:8-9), or on the road to Emmaus (Luke 24:13-15)?

- Did the resurrected Jesus first appear to the remaining eleven apostles in Galilee (Matthew 28:16-17) or in Jerusalem (Luke 24:33-36)?

- Was Jesus the first person ever to rise from the dead (Acts 26:23, Revelations 1:5) or not (1 Kings 17:17-24, 2 Kings 4:32-35, Matthew 9:23-25, Mark 6:35-42, Luke 7:12-15, Luke 8:49-55, John 11:43)?

There are many more contradictions in subsequent sections of the New Testament, but since Jesus's death and resurrection is a tough act to follow, and since this list is not meant to be exhaustive, we will stop there. That should suffice.

There are also blatant scientific errors in the Bible. Some insects are said to have four legs (Leviticus 11:20) when everyone knows they have six. Bats are categorized as a kind of bird (Leviticus 11:13-19) when most school children today could tell you they are in fact mammals. Math geeks have noted that the value of pi is misstated in the Bible as three rather than 3.14159265... (I Kings 7:23). Jesus himself appears to claim that the mustard seed is the smallest of seeds (Matthew 13: 31-32, Mark 4:30-32), when smaller seeds clearly exist in nature (e.g., certain orchid seeds are so small they are invisible to the naked eye); he also supposedly refers to the mustard plant as a tree that shelters birds (Luke 13:18-19) when it is more like a tall bush that only infrequently attracts nesting activity.

Additional examples of scientific error exist, along with geographical errors, historical errors, and more, but you get the idea. The Bible still gets most Christians around where they need to go, but as the flawless word of God it has more than a few dents in its fenders, the tire tread is getting a bit low, and it long ago lost that new car smell.

So you should now be well equipped to defend yourself should someone confront you with the ludicrous idea of biblical inerrancy, or the notion that the Bible is perfect in every way. These abundant examples of how laughably and manifestly wrong that concept is should be more than enough to break the spirit of even the shrillest, most obstinate and unthinking Fundamentalist.

The Second Fallacy: The Virgin Mary.

The story of the virgin birth of Jesus that appears in the Gospels of Matthew and Luke is anything but unique to Christianity. Tales of the immaculate conceptions of larger-than-life figures throughout history include: Chinese philosopher and author of the *Tao Te Ching* Lao Tzu; Gilagamesh the man-god Sumerian king and star of the *Epic of Gilgamesh*; Zoroaster, aka Zarathustra; Siddhartha Gautama, aka the Buddha, Hinduism's Krishna; the ancient Egyptian deity Horus (son of Isis); the Greek god Dionysus, and even Greek philosopher and mathematician Plato.

There are many others as well. Perhaps it's just a coincidence that all of those tales just named predate the birth of Jesus, perhaps not. Does it even matter? From the standpoint of comparative mythology, no credit is given for getting there first. In fact the recurrence of these themes only helps them resonate more powerfully. Looking back, one really ought to see the virgin birth motif as a mythical tribute involving the willing suspension of disbelief, comparable to a nomination for sainthood today, with its attendant compulsory miracle.

OK, but just because the concept of the Virgin Mary seems patterned after the mothers of prior religious figures, that doesn't prove it's a fabrication, does it? No, it doesn't. But here's what does: *the Bible*. Each of the four gospels, the book of Acts, and the letter of Paul to the Galatians all make explicit references to the siblings of Jesus, which, despite the Church's tortured excuse-making, remains very convincing evidence to anyone who can read that the idea of Mary's virginity, at least the *perpetual* aspect of it so vital to Mary cultists, is an obvious falsehood. Jesus had four brothers, named in the Bible: James, Joseph, Simon, and Judas (a popular name then, not so much now). He also had at least two sisters (and probably more) whom the Bible does not bother to name. Even the noted first century Roman historian Titus Flavius Josephus corroborated the existence of Jesus's brother, James, a prominent leader in the early Christian Church in Jerusalem. As historical questions go, this is proof beyond a reasonable doubt.

Here, with biblical citations and my italics, are the various references, the first three of which are obviously parallel versions of a single story echoing through the three Synoptic Gospels:

> While he [Jesus] was still speaking to the people, behold, *his mother and his brothers stood outside*, asking to speak to him. But he replied to the man who told him, "Who is my mother, and who are my brothers?" And stretching out his hand toward his disciples, he said, "Here are my mother and my brothers! For whoever does the will of my Father in heaven is my brother, and sister, and mother." (Matthew 12:46-50)

> And *his* [Jesus's] *mother and his brothers came*; and standing outside they sent to him and called him. And a crowd was sitting about him; and they said to him, "Your mother and your brothers are outside asking for you." And he replied, "Who are my mother and my brothers?" And looking around on those who sat about him, he said, "Here are my mother and my brothers! Whoever does the will of God is my brother, and sister, and mother." (Mark 3:31-35)

> Then *his mother and his brothers came* to him [Jesus], but they could not reach him for the crowd. And he was told, "Your mother and your brothers are standing outside, desiring to see you." But he said to them, "My mother and my brothers are those who hear the word of God and do it." (Luke 8:19-21)

> "Is not this the carpenter's son? Is not his mother called Mary? And are not *his brothers James and Joseph and Simon and Judas*? And are not *all his sisters* with us? Where then did this man get all this?" And they took offense at

him. But Jesus said to them, "A prophet is not without honor except in his own country and in his own house." (Matthew 13:55-57)

Now the Jews' feast of Tabernacles was at hand. So *his brothers said to him*, "Leave here and go to Judea, that your disciples may see the works you are doing. For no man works in secret if he seeks to be known openly. If you do these things, show yourself to the world." For even *his brothers* did not believe in him...But after *his brothers* had gone up to the feast [in Judea], then he also went up, not publicly but in private. (John 7:2-5, 10)

All these [apostles] with one accord devoted themselves to prayer, together with the women and Mary the mother of Jesus, and with *his brothers*. (Acts 1:14)

Then after three years I went up to Jerusalem to visit Cephas [Peter], and remained with him fifteen days. But I saw none of the other apostles except James *the Lord's brother*. In what I am writing to you, before God, I do not lie! (Galatians 1:18-20)

When Joseph woke from sleep, he did as the angel of the Lord commanded him; he took his wife [Mary], but *he knew her* [that is, had intercourse with her] *not until she had borne a son*; and he called his name Jesus. (Matthew 1:25)

Which clearly implies that afterward he *did* "know" her. And finally:

...so he [Ananus] assembled the sanhedrin of judges, and brought before them *the brother of Jesus*, who was called Christ, whose name was James, and some others;

and when he had formed an accusation against them as breakers of the law, he delivered them to be stoned... (Josephus's *Antiquities* 20.9.1, written in 94 A.D.)

So there it is, plain as day. And there's not a lot more that needs to be added. Mary was exactly as much a perpetual virgin as your own mother was. Which is to say: she was a virgin inside your head only, because you couldn't bear to think of her otherwise. Sadly, the Catholic and Eastern Churches likewise cannot bear to think of Mary any other way. But this book is not concerned with the careful maintenance of frail, patently untrue legends. So just as you were forced, at some point, to imagine the terrible reality of your own moment of conception, so too must these Churches and their followers face this fact: Mary was a real woman and a real mother.

Who knows? Perhaps Mary was the greatest woman and mother ever, to raise such a child, but she was a real mother nonetheless. Some historians even speculate that she was a *single* mother, as Joseph is mentioned by name in only two of the four gospels, and featured only in the context of the two dubious, conflicting birth narratives. Not only that but in a third gospel (John) Jesus pauses on the way to the cross to entrust the care of his mother to his beloved disciple without any explanation of why a married woman would need such help, and Joseph is also curiously absent from the first three Bible passages cited above, in which Jesus is told only that "his mother and his brothers" want to see him. So Mary may well have been a lot like many of you, women readers. Some might find great comfort in that.

But here's the rub: breaking this news to members of the Virgin Mary cult is not only as easy as proving that the shopping mall Santa is fake, it can also be just as unsatisfying. So I recommend going easy. One need only look at the iconography of these faiths to see the immense, grossly exaggerated importance of their beloved Virgin Mary myth. Now, a cynic might say a trick so sinister and so coldly calculated to win over pagan cultures accustomed to goddess deities doesn't deserve the kid glove treatment. But take my word for it. Win this easy victory over a Mary cultist, savor the silence it brings you, and move on.

The Third Fallacy: The "Born Again" Concept

Perhaps nothing is quite as tiresome and annoying in the Fundamentalist Christians' repertoire as their ultimate trump card: the "born again" speech. This is the unanswerable assertion that if only you, the rational non-Fundamentalist, would accept Jesus Christ as your Lord and savior and open yourself up to magical thinking, you too might experience the rapture of being "born again" and the miracle of an accompanying variety of supernatural Christian phenomena.

There are a number of problems with this. One of the more obvious ones, though it is imperceptible to many Christians, is that the world is filled with non-Christians likewise claiming to have supernatural abilities, from gypsy fortune tellers to psychic mediums to Indian shamans to voodoo doctors to Eastern mystics to Las Vegas showmen. Not only that, but almost every one of the world's religions lays claim to some connection with supernatural phenomena, leaving them all tied for both first and last places in the race to convince nonbelievers. In other words, making the claim isn't the least bit extraordinary. That's because any conceivable claim of supernatural power means nothing, and *ought to* mean nothing, without an empirical demonstration. So where is yours, Mr. Evangelical? And why should I believe that your power comes from Jesus and not from Satan, whose supernatural powers you oddly find just as real?

While we are on this subject, snobbish Fundamentalists, my refusal to accept *your* impervious bloviating on supernatural phenomena does *not* mean I fail to perceive a metaphysical dimension to the experience of being human. Not at all. But I digress, because there is yet another far larger problem with the idea of being "born again," namely that the whole concept is the result of a biblical misquote. Yes.

Do words matter? In a religion based on a book, they ought to, and according to biblical scholars the key phrase in the familiar passage from the Gospel of John 3:3—"Verily, verily, I say unto thee, Except a man be born again, he cannot see the kingdom of God," the source of the "born again" concept—represents a mistranslation of what Jesus said. In the oldest and best surviving copies of the Gospel of John, written in ancient Greek, this oft-quoted verse uses the Greek word *anothen*, meaning "from above," not *gennao*, the word for "again" (or "anew"), in connection with the Greek word for birth. "Again" is at best an obscure secondary meaning of *anothen*.

So "again" is possible then, right? Wrong. Consider that, apart from when Jesus quickly echoes himself in verse seven, every single other time that the word *anothen* occurred in ancient Greek biblical manuscripts it was translated as "from above," not as "again." That includes another example appearing at the end of that very same chapter of John. At John 3:31 Jesus is quoted as saying "He that cometh from above [*anothen*] is above all; he that is of the earth is earthly, and speaketh of the earth; he that cometh from heaven is above all."

The historical motivation of John's later translators for choosing "again" for verses three and seven and *only* for them is a subject experts continue to debate today. But it is obvious from this later passage in the same conversation that whatever Jesus was trying to get across to the Pharisee Nicodemus in John 3:3, it was not the idea of being born *again*. Rather, it was a reference to some kind of vertical, heavenly (as opposed to earthly) birth. Therefore the "born again" concept is a misprint, a *faux pas*, a blooper, a translator fail. But, believe it or not, that's not even the worst part for born-again Christians. Why? Because, as we have seen time and again, there is yet another layer of controversy to this Christian tradition. Allow me to explain.

Now pay close attention for a second. Here is the exact exchange between Nicodemus and Jesus, beginning at John 3:2, using the translation biblical scholars prefer:

> Rabbi, we know that thou art a teacher come from God: for no one can do these miracles that thou doest, except God be with him.

Jesus answered and said to him, "Verily, verily, I say to unto thee, Except a man be born from above [*anothen*] he cannot see the kingdom of God."

Nicodemus saith to him, "How can a man be born when he is old? Can he enter a second time into his mother's womb, and be born?"

Now looking at this one could certainly argue, as those favoring the "born again" construction have long done, that Nicodemus seems to understand this as born *again* (he even says "enter a second time")—a confusion Jesus later addresses in verse thirty-one (quoted above) by contrasting earthly things and "heavenly" things, supporting a "birth *from above*" construction. So Jesus is attempting to clear up any misunderstanding about which of the two definitions of *anothen* he meant, right? Wrong, because here's the thing: this ambiguity occurs only in Greek, the language of the original written gospel of John. Nicodemus and Jesus both spoke Aramaic, a language in which the ambiguity simply does not exist. So however you translate *anothen*, it must have meant the exact same thing to Jesus as it did to Nicodemus. Oops! Born again? More like fooled again.

Given this background, how can this exchange between the two, based on the idea of a problem with a double entendre that Nicodemus took the wrong way, then a clarification by Jesus, how can it possibly be looked at without some measure of skepticism about its authenticity if the problem *didn't even exist* in the native language of the speakers? And how does this dubious exchange end? With no less a finale than the single best-known verse in the entire Bible: the iconic John 3:16.

Do words matter? Let me ask you something. Would it matter if the Lord's Prayer began "Our Mother, who art in heaven..."? So tell me again, duped Fundamentalist, about your experience of being born... *from above*.

The Fourth Fallacy: The Holy Trinity

As referenced above and detailed below, the Christian doctrine of the Holy Trinity is spelled out in its defining creeds, including primarily the Nicene Creed, composed at the Turkish town of Nicea starting in 325 A.D. There is one god made up of three gods who are different but the same. In theological terms they are three hypostases in one ousia (three distinct essences in one irreducible being), though it must be stated that theologians could split hairs for an eternity over the precise meaning of language in this context.

Here's what you need to know when a Fundamentalist rube gets in your face: this concept of a triune god cannot be found in their Bible, it just can't, not anywhere, although an attempt was made to plant it there. That's right. This most central of beliefs for most Christians, the idea that the god they pray to each night is rightly conceived of as the Father, the Son, and the Holy Spirit does not plainly appear anywhere in the book that is their ultimate authority on all things Christian.

How in the world is this possible? Well, as any exasperating Fundamentalist will be happy to tell you, with God *all things are possible!*

The truth is that nobody knows exactly when the concept of the Holy Trinity made its way into Christian dogma. Nobody even claims to know. But to give one telling example, there is nothing in the letters of Saint Paul, who was not the least bit bashful about defining proper belief, indicating he taught it as doctrine in the earliest days of the church.

The oldest surviving explicit reference to the Trinity is a passage from the Catholic ecclesiastical writer Tertullian from sometime in the early third century: "the very Church itself is, properly and principally, the Spirit Himself, in whom is the Trinity of the One Divinity—Father, Son, and Holy Spirit." (From *On Pudicity,* chapter twenty one.)

But even that is a bit shaky. The church *is* the Holy Spirit? And the Trinity is *in* the Holy Spirit even though it *includes* the Holy Spirit?

Obviously the terminology still needed some work, but by the time church poobahs assembled in Nicea roughly a hundred years later (as described in part one of this book), the idea of the Holy Trinity had somehow gained widespread acceptance. The council used it as the framework for the Nicene Creed, and that, ladies and gentlemen, was that.

In the centuries that followed, it was understood that to question the Trinity doctrine was not just an affront to Catholic orthodoxy, it was an affront to the authority of the Church to declare it. Even today, a Catholic encyclopedia tersely puts it like this:

> It is manifest that a dogma so mysterious [as the Trinity] presupposes a divine revelation. When the fact of a revelation, understood in its full sense as the speech of God to man, is no longer admitted, the rejection of the doctrine follows as a necessary consequence. (The Catholic Encyclopedia: An International Work of Reference on the Constitution, Doctrine, Discipline, and History of the Catholic Church, Volume 15, page 47)

In other words, it is obvious that anything *that* hard to understand *must* come from God, which is exactly why you must believe it. Well then! That is certainly a trump card that cannot be played often, and a more circuitous tautology you will never find. But thank you for that snarky concession to logic at the end, Catholic Encyclopedia!

Looking back, it appears we can safely say that 1) Christians originally believed in the doctrine of the Trinity simply because the Church told them to in the mid-fourth century, and 2) they believe it today because they have believed it for so long. And while there is a smattering of Bible verses suggestive of a triune god, there are just as many quoting Jesus describing his role as subordinate to the Father. For example, in Matthew 24:36, while speaking to his disciples about end times, he said, "But of that day and hour no one knows, not even the angels of heaven, nor the Son, but the Father only." In John 14:28 he tells them, "You have heard me say to you, 'I go away, and I will come to you.' If you loved me, you would have rejoiced, because I go to the Father; for the Father is greater than I." Perhaps most telling of all, in Mark 10:17-18, "a man ran up and knelt before him, and asked him, 'Good Teacher, what must I do to inherit eternal life?' And Jesus said to him, 'Why do you call me good? No one is good but God alone.'"

That, my friends, is simply not the kind of talk you would expect from an omnipotent, omniscient co-equal deity present at the creation of the universe. But who among us has the right to question the re-vealed truths of the Roman Catholic Church, you ask? Well, if you are a Protestant, your denomination was founded on the very principle that *you* do. That's who.

Could this story get any worse for Christians in search of solid ground for their belief in a triune god? Once again it could, because on closer inspection, the doctrine of the Holy Trinity proves suspicious in other ways, the most embarrassing of which is the controversial role played by the so-called Johannine Comma in its history. And just what in the heck is the Johannine Comma? I'm glad you asked. But before I get to it, let's back up a bit.

In the first part of this book, we talked about how the Bible as it is known today, with its New and Old Testaments and its collection of sixty-six total books, came into being in the late fourth century. But we were talking about the selection of its named books and their arrangement, not the word-for-word text of those books. At the time, that was far from settled or uniform.

Let's back up a little further. From around 50 A.D., when Paul's influential epistles began circulating, through the following half century or so when the four gospels were written, until the conversion of Emperor Constantine around 312 A.D., the hand-written Greek manuscripts of the books of the Bible were for the most part being produced only haphazardly by amateur copyists. They were making copies from random other copies because the originals of all these books were either disappearing or already gone. As a result, many variations—some accidental, some deliberate, most of them insignificant, a few quite important—could be found in the text of those early manuscripts. Still more crept in when the first attempts were made to translate the original Greek into the more familiar Latin language of Western Europe.

As the Church had yet to take a formal stand on which of these slightly different versions ought to be considered true, Pope Damasus in the late fourth century asked the venerable scholar Jerome to produce an official Latin translation using Greek manuscripts supplied by the Vatican. This he did, and it included the following passage with my italics, later dubbed the Johannine Comma:

> *There are three that bear witness in heaven; the Father, the Word* [aka Jesus], *and the Spirit, and these three are one;* and there are three that bear witness on earth, the Spirit, the water, and the blood, and those three are one. (1 John 5:7-8)

The first part, my friends, was and is the only relatively unambiguous statement of the Trinity doctrine in the entire Bible, period. And it does not appear in the oldest and arguably most authentic Greek manuscripts.

The Church accepted Jerome's translation of the Bible, commonly known as the Latin Vulgate, as the last word on the subject for more than a thousand years, during which time precious little was done to compare its contents to the best ancient manuscripts that surfaced. In fact the original Greek of the New Testament mostly faded from Western memory until the early 1500s, after Gutenberg's invention of the printing press, when scholarly interest in printing a Greek Bible started to build. The first one to circulate, put together by the Dutch intellectual Desiderius Erasmus in 1515 and based on a fairly random collection of old manuscripts, did not contain the Johannine Comma. When a righteous outcry over its omission ensued, Erasmus promised he would re-insert it on the condition that his critics produce a hand-written Greek manuscript that included it. No problem! The Church, rather than scour through archives for an ancient one, apparently had copyists fabricate a new one just for the occasion, and right back into the Bible the Johannine Comma went (but with a lengthy footnote from Erasmus expressing his fear that the source for it was inauthentic). That's right, you heard me: modern scholars believe the Church in Rome supplied Erasmus with a fake Greek manuscript just to get back its Holy Trinity doctrine.

The authority of Erasmus's final edition, thus altered, was so widely accepted it became known as the *Textus Receptus*—the text received by all. Moreover, the English language King James Version of the Bible so beloved by your grandparents and forefathers was translated and published based largely upon it in 1611. For English-speaking Christianity over the past four hundred years no higher authority on the contents of the Bible could possibly be named. Yet the foundational *Textus Receptus* contained passages not appearing in or supported by many of the oldest and best Greek manuscripts available in its time, including the epilogue at the end of Mark described in part one of this book, the story from John of the accused adulteress* ("let he who is without sin cast the first stone"), and yes, the much-ballyhooed Johannine Comma. All of them were ultimately included in the *Textus Receptus* based in part on a fake manuscript, authenticity be damned.

So once again we clearly see fingerprints all over Christian theology, and they don't belong to Jesus or even to his apostles. If your tormentors aren't aware of this chink in their Fundamentalist armor, well, this would seem like the perfect time to bring it up. Because how could you or anyone trust Christians who add or subtract from their Holy Bible to support a theology Jesus himself never articulated? Right, proselytizing clod who doesn't even know where his own faith came from? Am I right?

*It is truly a great pity that such a delightful story perhaps ought to be considered inauthentic... (sigh).

The Fifth Fallacy: The Relevance of the Old Testament

You might ask yourself from time to time—What is the go-to source for biblical quotations when a Fundamentalist freak is making homophobic signs to wave in front of his local Chick-fil-A restaurant? As already alluded to in part one of this book, it is none other than the slightly modified Jewish Tanakh, appended to the front of the Christian Bible and known as the Old Testament.

Was it ever thus? Have Christians always reached for their Old Testament when they wanted to justify action in direct opposition to the teachings of Jesus? The answer, sadly, is yes, but things could have turned out much differently.

Who out there knows who Marcion is? Anybody? I dropped a hint earlier. Nobody? OK, here's some help. Marcion of Sinope, born in 85 A.D. in what is now Turkey, was a Catholic bishop and hugely influential writer who, operating in the relative theological vacuum of the early Church, proposed something quite amazing: that Yahweh, the god of the Jews, and Jesus, the god of two billion people today, were not one single god, were not two of three different hypostases in one ousia, but rather two separate gods in complete opposition to one another. Now I know what you're saying—there's no way a bishop and important early Church leader espoused anything that wild, that weird, that whacky. But think again.

Recall that we just learned how Christianity went almost three hundred years before deciding that it believed in a triune God. So yes, to put it bluntly, the well-known early Church leader Marcion *did indeed* teach that there was a jealous, petty, vengeful god following around a small, nomadic tribe of Semitic herdsmen, and a rival, superior, benevolent god represented on Earth by Jesus, who came here as a cosmic world savior to bring enlightenment to the human race through his message of love and compassion.

Actually, when you stop and really think about it for a second, stop and think hard…this alternative version of the story doesn't sound that crazy at all. Does it?

The real truth is that Marcion's take on Christianity—that Jesus's life, death, and resurrection eclipsed and replaced Judaism—hardly does more violence to the story found in the four gospels than does Christian orthodoxy. Remember that before the emergence of Saint Paul, Christianity was floundering around as a cult of Jewish heretics, keeping the Sabbath and offering animal sacrifices, waiting for an imminent apocalypse of some kind or another. Remember that Judaism's distinguishing feature among religions of that era was its strict monotheism, the belief in a single, all-powerful god. It was Yahweh or the highway for the Jews; no provision was made in their theology for a literal son of God (much less a Holy Spirit) sharing that role, because that would have been *blasphemy!*

What's more, Jesus's followers were still stuck in old, prophetic definitions of the Messiah, and struggling to reconcile two deeply conflicting things: their dream of seeing the charismatic military leader of Jewish prophecy who would, in the tradition of the great King David, blah blah blah, you remember the shtick, and the clashing reality of Jesus's crucifixion, which epitomized their continuing powerlessness.

At least until Saint Paul came around. Paul grabbed the reins and steered the Church toward what it is today. Paul welcomed in the Gentiles. Paul articulated the meaning of Jesus's death. Paul supplied the formula for atonement and salvation. Paul, Paul, Paul. It was Paul who served as the architect of true Christian faith, not Marcion. So who was Marcion citing as the authority for his outrageous claim that Judaism and the Torah were dead?

You guessed it: Saint Paul. And he had good reasons for doing so. Marcion also cited an even higher authority—Jesus—claiming that parables such as the ones advising against patching an old garment with new cloth, or putting new wine in old wineskins, were meant to support his view of complete replacement (see Matthew 9:16-17). A better explanation for those enigmatic parables you will frankly not find.

Believe it or not, the Marcionite movement gained enormous traction, and although Vatican officials ex-communicated him around 144

A.D., an impressive number of churches remained loyal to him, even breaking away from Rome to follow his teachings. In fact this Marcionite strain of Christianity even survived its own founder's attempts to make peace with Rome and persisted for three hundred years.

These Marcionites were also among the earliest Christians to select a biblical canon of books, which for them was a version of the gospel of Luke (presumably altered somewhat to minimize Jewish prophecy) and ten of the letters attributed to Paul. Needless to say it included no Old Testament. Historians believe that the Church in Rome's subsequent effort to select an official biblical canon was undertaken partly in response to this. Some of them also suspect it was Marcion who first collected Paul's letters back when it was still possible to do so, placing the Church deeply in his debt. This is not the only sense in which the Church is indebted to him. One could honestly say the eventual shape of Christianity was in large part a reaction *against* Marcionism. So it was a considerable force, was.

What happened? The same thing happened that always happens when temporary forces have the temerity to stand in the Vatican's way. The Roman Church soldiered on in opposition to Marcionite beliefs across centuries, and like a tree trunk that envelopes an adjacent wrought-iron fence over a vast period of time, the Church gradually accommodated and ultimately absorbed the blatant inconsistencies between the Old and New Testaments. Then it started pretending they don't even exist (though clearly they do). Which brings us to today, when even the most fervent Christian is often plagued by a small voice in his head asking: *How do I reconcile this square peg with that round hole?*

I have news: it can't be done. Christian faith revolves around a triune god and a biune philosophy. Blessed are the peacemakers—until it's time to wage war. Love your enemies—unless they believe differently from you. Judge not—except you may judge sexual preference, and so on, and so on.

This insistence on clinging to the Old Testament as a guide to being Christian is really quite astonishing when one considers that Paul, a Jew and by far the most influential person outside of Jesus in the entire history of Christianity, described Jewish Law as a "ministry of death, chiseled in letters on a stone tablet" (an apparent reference to nothing less than the beloved Ten Commandments) that should be replaced by "a ministry of the Spirit come in glory" (2 Corinthians 3:7-8). That sounds a lot like Marcion. Not stopping there, Paul referred to Jewish practitioners of circumcision, as "dogs and evildoers" who "mutilate the flesh" (Philippians 3:2). This coming from a self-described "Hebrew born of Hebrews" and a "Pharisee" (Philippians 3:5-6) regarding perhaps the single most sacred rite in Judaism!

In the end two irreconcilable things seem certain: 1) the shape of modern Christianity is largely the creation of Saint Paul, and 2) Paul, after his conversion, wanted little or nothing to do with Judaism or Hebrew scriptures, the Christian Old Testament. If you doubt me, oh Fundamentalist fruit loop, read that last paragraph again. Then go inside and console yourself with a chicken sandwich.

The Pharisees were experts in Jewish law who, along with the so-called scribes (or literate copyists), were considered to be among the Jews most devoted to their religion. However, they received some of Jesus's most scathing criticisms for what he considered their intolerable hypocrisy.

PART THREE

KNOW THY CHRISTIAN ENEMY

Let's say your new girlfriend's family has invited you to Christmas dinner. No problem, you love home cooking. But then she goes to church with them on Christmas Eve—you beg off to watch football in secret—so now you know there's a chance that the conversation tomorrow could go...*there*. How do you get ready in time? And what are you getting ready for?

No worries! Here is a quick look at the basic tenets of Christianity, along with a breakdown of the similarities and differences between the Roman Catholic Church and various popular Protestant churches (or denominations). As a public service, I have included a rating of how crazy each one is, so your internal Geiger counter will know when to start ticking. The section closes with a few words about humanity's other leading faiths.

Why are these details important? Because it might astonish you how weak a grasp most Christians have on their own theology and its place among world religions, and embarrassing them about their ignorance may be just the distraction you need to make a clean getaway. Just remember to wait until *after* you've had her mom's famous bourbon pecan pie.

Christianity

The big kahuna. It is probably best to simply start with the Nicene Creed, referenced in the first section of this book. Bear in mind that minor differences in the precise language of this creed occur throughout Christianity.

We believe in one God, the Father Almighty, maker of heaven and earth, and of all things, visible and invisible; and in one Lord Jesus Christ, the only-begotten Son of God, begotten of the Father before all worlds, God of God, Light of Light, Very God of Very God, begotten, not made, being of one substance with the Father by whom all things were made, who for us men, and for our salvation, came down from heaven, and was incarnate by the Holy Spirit of the Virgin Mary, and was made man, and was crucified also for us under Pontius Pilate. He suffered and was buried, and on the third day he rose again according to the scriptures, and ascended into heaven, and sitteth at the right hand of the Father. And he shall come again with glory to judge both the quick and the dead, whose kingdom shall have no end.

And we believe in the Holy Ghost, the Lord and Giver of Life, who proceedeth from the Father and the Son, who with the Father and the Son together is worshipped and glorified, who spake by the prophets. And we believe in one holy catholic and apostolic Church. We acknowledge one baptism for the remission of sins. And we look for the resurrection of the dead, and the life of the world to come. Amen.

FYI, in this context, "catholic and apostolic" is meant to convey the idea of a universal, commissioned church.

The other recitation of faith well known to most Christians is the Apostles' Creed, which is of uncertain origin, and which, like its cousin the Nicene Creed, exists in a variety of slightly altered versions.

I believe in God the Father Almighty, maker of heaven and earth.

And in Jesus Christ, his only Son, our Lord, who was conceived by the Holy Spirit, born of the Virgin Mary, suffered under Pontius Pilate, was crucified, died and was buried. He descended into hell. On the third day He rose again from the dead. He ascended into heaven and sits at the right hand of the God the Father Almighty. From thence he will come to judge the living and the dead.

I believe in the Holy Ghost, the holy Christian Church, the communion of saints, the forgiveness of sins, the resurrection of the body, and the life everlasting. Amen.

While they aren't exactly locked in mortal conflict, there are some very clear differences of language and emphasis between the two creeds. Perhaps the most interesting detail from the latter is the notion that after Jesus's death he *literally went straight to hell* before bobbing back up into heaven.

In any case, there you have it: Christianity in a nutshell. And it turns out to be basically as advertised in part one of this book—triune God with creator Father, savior Son (of a virgin), inspiring Spirit, and eternal life for true believers. Now let's break down some of the different forms of Christianity, because the devil, as they say, is in the details, and you'd better believe it pays to know your enemy when you are faced with a full frontal Fundamentalist assault.

Catholicism versus Protestantism

This distinction could fill entire books and has, but I will try to keep it simple here. Catholics believe that the Church in Rome, guided by the Holy Spirit, is the proper interpreter of the Bible, while most Protestants don't recognize their Church as a divine institution with the authority to dictate belief. They believe instead that the Church takes the form of a fellowship of believers whose access to the Bible is their principal guide. By contrast, Roman Catholics (and Eastern Orthodox) believe that God's message filters down to the individual after being distilled by the institution of the Church, which enjoys a kind of divine protection from error that no individual Christian could ever hope to match.

There are a great many other differences both profound and trivial, theological and ministerial, but this one is the most basic: Catholics are supposed to believe and do as the Church dictates. Protestants are to a much greater degree allowed to follow the dictates of their own hearts and minds. What follows is a summary of different Protestant denominations, along with a Sanctimometer© ranking for each one. This is a rough measurement of the tendency of each to discourage independent thinking, to foster hateful attitudes, to judge alternative lifestyles, or to indulge in displays of public piety—in other words, to act like sanctimonious jackasses.

Note as we go that the division of each branch of Protestantism into even smaller sub-groups often results from differences of opinion on how crazy its members want to act along exactly these same lines.

Lutheran

This denomination can legitimately lay claim to the title of being the original Protestant Church. Lutheranism preserves more of the liturgy (the script of a church service), vestments (priestly garb), church calendar, décor, and architecture of the Catholic Church than most other Protestant denominations. The features that distinguished it from Catholicism were its emphasis on individual Bible study and Luther's staunch opposition to good works or deeds as part of the formula for being saved. He instead claimed Christians are justified to God purely by grace. In other words they are lucky bastards whom God accepts despite their flaws if they simply repent and believe. Also, it helps to be baptized. These are the recurring themes of Protestantism generally.

Owing perhaps to its origins, Lutheranism is a comparatively intellectual denomination. In general its Sanctimometer© reading is **low** crazy, although there are divisions within Lutheranism, called synods, ranking medium (Missouri Synod) to high (Wisconsin Synod). Most Lutheran groups ordain women, encourage higher education, are fairly tolerant of homosexuals (the largest synod now ordains non-celibate gays), rarely pander to the media, and have little historical association with racism in this country.

Presbyterian

Named after its representative, decentralized organizational unit, the presbytery, this denomination's adherents historically followed the teachings of John Calvin (aka Jean Cauvin), a French lawyer-turned-reformer who was a contemporary of Martin Luther. Classic Calvinism, it has to be said, was a very harsh thing indeed. All music and art were stripped from the worship experience; mankind was declared totally depraved because Eve had bitten the apple; and, most disturbing of all, the church taught that God predetermines who will be saved and who will be eternally damned. Official doctrine unapologetically undermined the role of free will, imagining that if necessary God could force those to sin whom he had marked for hell. The prominent eighteenth century Presbyterian theologian Jonathan Edwards, grandfather of Aaron Burr, once proclaimed that "Hell is paved with the skulls of unbaptized children." *Riiight!*

To its credit the church has greatly moderated its position on most of these issues, though perhaps it had little choice. Modern Presbyterianism, while still basically conservative, has evolved into something far more contemporary. Its theology is highly communal. It encourages education, thrift, and philanthropy and is pro-capitalist. As a result its members tend on average to be fairly wealthy, influential, and middle to upper class.

Although the largest US Presbyterian group has approved the ordination of non-celibate gays, the church remains fairly divided on the issue of homosexuality. In fairness, however, so are most churches, and

Presbyterianism generally registers a **medium-to-low** crazy reading on the Sanctimometer©. It doesn't foment much hatred or indulge in a great deal of media grandstanding, but unsurprisingly, a nineteenth century north-south schism in American Calvinism had a racial component, with Southerners upset over the Northern branch's liberalism and opposition to slavery. Sound familiar?

Methodist

Younger than most Protestant denominations, the Methodist Church was founded in the eighteenth century by go-getter John Wesley, who was originally an ordained Anglican priest and failed missionary to the British colony of Georgia. Thought by many historians to be a natural born entrepreneur who under different circumstances might've started a restaurant chain or a dot-com, he instead started a new church after becoming disillusioned with the stoicism of the Church of England. Wesley believed in sudden, spontaneous conversion through the Holy Spirit, and Methodism at one time expected each of its members to testify to such a moment. He also believed in free will and insisted on the need for good works. As a result, Methodism is a practical, activist faith, more concerned with evangelism than theological reflection. Most of its members reside in the United States and come primarily from the middle to upper-middle class. The biggest group, the United Methodist Church (UMC), was formed by a 1968 merger of two smaller units and is arguably the most highly organized religious body in American Christianity outside of the Catholic Church.

Wesley's emphasis on good works has at times yielded fruit. The Methodist Church established Goodwill Industries in 1907 to aid the handicapped and it has a respectable record on most civil rights issues of race and gender. However, the Church's position on homosexuality is extremely disappointing. Recent official church rhetoric that deigns to reaffirm the basic human worth of gays while at the same time condemning homosexuality as incompatible with Christian teaching is halfhearted and weak, to say the least. The same withered olive branch could logically be held out to pedophiles and serial killers. Of course the ordination of homosexuals is forbidden. This official policy of discrimination, when added to a blue-nosed Church history that includes sobriety oaths and bans on dancing, card playing, and tobacco use, earns Methodism a **medium** Sanctimometer© rating.

Episcopalian

This is the American version of the Church of England, or Anglican Church, created by King Henry VIII to facilitate his divorce, as described earlier. In theory it is both Catholic and Protestant, as well as neither, claiming to resist the "additions of Catholicism and the subtractions of Protestantism." In practice it is very close to Catholicism, but stubbornly refuses to acknowledge the supremacy of Rome and its pope. Its members tend to be fairly wealthy, buttoned-down, and well-connected. Its rolls include many former US presidents and VIPs. Like nearly all other denominations, it is highly subdivided. It somehow manages to exist in three forms: High Church (very Catholic), Low Church (more Protestant), and Broad Church (mixed).

Despite the Episcopalian Church's resemblance to Catholicism on many levels, its social policies tend to be quite liberal. It has what is, by comparison to some other denominations, a fairly proud history of reaching out to people of color (though Southern bishops during the Civil War did organize a Confederate branch of the Church that dissolved back into the main body after the Civil War). It has long ordained women. Its pioneering embrace of tolerance for homosexuality and the ordination of gays has come at a high price, causing a great deal of church splintering, litigation, and discord as well as a loss of membership. It deserves credit for this and for its nuanced position on abortion, and thus earns a **low** Sanctimometer© reading.

Baptist

And the needle on the Sanctimometer© jumps. The Baptist Church in its diverse forms is the largest of American Protestant denominations. Concentrated mostly in the American South, Baptists represent a substantial majority of church members in ten of the eleven states of the former Confederacy.

As the name suggests, the rite of adult baptism by immersion is a central focus of the movement. In their theology, the Baptists took the Protestant Reformation a step further, abolishing infant baptism, all creeds, all sacraments, hierarchical church government, and many worship rituals they considered non-biblical.

The Baptist tradition of ferocious resistance to vertical authority, while admirable in theory, has helped produce individual Baptist congregations so painfully backward they threaten to shatter the Sanctimometer© to pieces—the Westboro Baptist Church of Topeka, Kansas, infamous for its homophobic protests at veteran funerals and other venues, serves as a prominent example. And in an irony for the ages, this historically racist denomination at least nominally has the largest African-American membership among all churches. In fact the Southern Baptist Convention, the largest of all Baptist associations, was founded in 1845 specifically as a pro-slavery counterweight to Northern abolitionists in the Church. More recently, white Baptists mostly watched the civil rights movement from the sidelines even though its spiritual leader, the Rev. Dr. Martin Luther King, Jr., was a Baptist minister. What's more, Baptists persist with positions on homosexuality that come almost unchanged from the nineteenth century.

While pandering to and shaking down their many poor adherents, Baptists have amassed enormous wealth and immense political power with ruthless efficiency, which they often wield to the profound socioeconomic harm of those same constituents. All of this they cynically do in direct logical contravention of the teachings of Jesus. To paraphrase the campfire hymn based on John 13:35, no one would ever know they are Christians by their love. The Baptist Church frankly deserves its own Sanctimometer© category, but out of respect for its many decent individual members, I will simply leave its rating at **high.**

Pentecostal/Assemblies of God

As one might guess from its name, this group, in which the Assemblies of God are the leading presence, is notable for its fixation on glossolalia, or speaking in tongues, said to be a gift of the Holy Spirit and first reported in the original Christian Pentecost from the book of Acts. For some reason glossolalia took about an eighteen hundred year break after visiting those earliest Christians, then emerged as a routine part of the Pentecostal experience. It is supposed to be evidence of one's salvation through adult baptism in the Holy Spirit.

Efforts to subject glossolalia to controlled study and linguistic analysis indicate the Pentecostal phenomenon is no more than an ecstatic fit in which the subjects, motivated by intense social pressure and religious fervor, generate nonsense syllables that crudely mimic human speech. Abundant examples exist on YouTube. Try not to laugh when you watch them. In fairness, a very small handful of cases that challenge scientific explanation do exist.

These churches are otherwise unremarkable in their basic theology, but they are homophobic, they consider the Bible inerrant, and their history includes bans on liquor, tobacco, dancing, certain haircuts, cosmetics, jewelry, labor unions, card playing, and movies. For this, and for shaming their youth into faking supernatural experiences that get posted on the Internet, these polyglot scat rappers merit a **high** Sanctimometer© rating.

Church of Christ

This denomination's rallying cry is "no creed but Christ," and they imagine themselves to be recreating the very earliest Christian churches, as they first existed in the immediate aftermath of Jesus's crucifixion. Of course to properly do *that*, they would have to become Jewish apocalypticists, but no matter.

They believe strongly in local church autonomy, but that local authority is vested in a shadowy, male-dominated hierarchy of elders, deacons, and laymen. They practice only adult baptism by immersion, and the music in their worship services must be strictly *a cappella*. Why? Because the New Testament makes no mention of musical instruments, that's why. Do they walk to church because the New Testament makes no mention of automobiles? No, but let's not confuse matters further.

The Church of Christ uses grape juice for Holy Communion, considers the Bible inerrant, and has a shaky history of race relations. Its attitude towards homosexuality is predictably harsh. It deserves a **high** Sanctimometer© rating.

United Church of Christ

This is an entirely different animal from the Churches of Christ, and one should never confuse the two. Formed by the merger of two dissimilar groups—the Congregationalists (with a Calvinist background) and the Evangelical and Reformed Church (with a Lutheran background)—the United Churchmen generally hold fairly progressive views toward civil rights issues, homosexuality, and reproductive rights. They ordain women as pastors and their theology tends to be fairly liberal. Of the Bible they say that "though written in specific historical times and places, [it] still speaks to us in our present condition." They are very ecumenical, meaning they communicate well with other denominations and faiths. In fact, they are members of the National Muslim-Christian Initiative.

They abhor any kind of vertical authority, and the relative autonomy of individual churches allows for a great deal of variability among parishes. Fortunately that principle, rather than being the license to explore fringe lunacy it is among certain Baptists, seems to give the United Churchmen a relaxed, non-doctrinaire quality that earns them a fairly **low** Sanctimometer© reading.

African-American churches

Of course it is grossly unfair and more than a bit ironic to lump these lively Christians together into one stereotype, but a few things about African-American churches deserve specific mention. First, their story is poignant, as the conversion of African slaves to Christianity in the United States was originally a slave-taming strategy, so to speak (see part four below). Because of this they are owed considerable leeway in how they choose to worship today.

Second, their worship experience has always emphasized the spiritual dimension, which contributes to the prominent role music plays in these churches. To state the exceedingly obvious, the world stands deeply in their debt for this rich cultural phenomenon. *The rest of the human race thanks you, African-American Christians, for the priceless gifts of spiritual music and its offspring—jazz, blues, and R&B.*

Third, while the theology of African-American churches has long leaned in a conservative direction, their members have, as a community, recently shown a remarkable capacity for recognizing the basic similarity of homophobia to racism and moved past it for the most part. For that they deserve praise and no worse than a **medium** Sanctimometer© rating.

Non-denominational

Almost any attempt to characterize this American church grouping—the eighth largest today—will depend on the individual congregation, as they are all by definition unaffiliated with a centralized Church body. Their membership swelled from fewer than two hundred thousand in the United States in 1990 to more than eight million by 2008. They bear names that betray the marketing savvy behind their operations—Crossroads, Fisherman's Home, New Creation, New Hope, New Frontiers, Next Level, Victory Christian, Vineyard Christian, Table of Grace, Tree of Life, World Changers. Although their independence provides them with virtually unlimited freedom to express a wide variety of Christian preferences, they nonetheless tend to gravitate toward conservative social and theological positions and, more than anything else, seem to share a penchant for slick self-promotion and extravagant enrichment of an inner circle of church organizers. This is especially true among the larger non-denominational churches.

While it is tempting to describe the adaptability of these churches in natural selection terms, it is more appropriate to use the language of the economic free market. They are run like nimble businesses because that's what they are, with many of them offering attendance incentives (free Starbucks!), generating massive social media activity, and monitoring online reviews with paid staff. They keep the customer satisfied by featuring glittering facilities and simple, user-friendly (some would say dumbed-down) worship formats as well as lots of feel-good fellowship. In fact, bloated pride and tingly togetherness are very big components of the nondenominational experience, and meditative introspection a very small part.

The brand is typified on the high end by mega-churches such as the one run by the best-selling author Joel Osteen. These institutions spend freely and go big. For example, while there is no way to know which Christian group leads the world in expensive Third World missions that place its members awkwardly in the way of actual relief organizations, thereby siphoning away donation money that might have literally saved lives, wealthy non-denominational churches would be a pretty good bet.

These churches' creepy, un-Christian focus on their economic bottom lines and their shameless, unrestrained use of the business model, combined with their over-the-top media presence, fondness for proselytizing, and generally anti-progressive positions on social and theological issues justify a solid **high** Sanctimometer© reading. Bear in mind, however, that by definition there is at least the potential for significant individual variation among them.

***

The following are Christian churches in some sense or another, but not what most theologians would consider Protestant in nature.

Eastern Orthodox

One might be tempted to think the Eastern Orthodox, not Lutherans, were the original Protestants, but from their perspective it was the Roman Catholic Church that abandoned Christianity's original pathway* and went astray. Still, the Church closely mirrors Catholicism in most respects. Like the Roman Catholic Church, it claims authority traceable to the original apostles. It is the predominant Christian denomination of Eastern Europe, Russia, and the Middle East. It differs from Roman Catholicism in a number of small ways concerning the nature of purgatory, doctrines related to Mary, and the like. It does not ordain women, and its formal policies toward reproductive rights and homosexuality are comparable to those of the Catholic Church—which is to say, terrible.

Although the Eastern Orthodox Church proselytizes comparatively little and boasts the best food in the church festival business, it merits a **medium-to-high** Sanctimometer© rating.

*According to religious scholar and author Philip Jenkins, it might have been the even more easterly ancient community of Christians in and around modern Syria and Iraq that hewed closest to the Church's original tenets and practices for many centuries. That little-understood branch of Christianity ultimately failed to survive the rise of Islam in the region, but the lengthy coexistence of the two faiths in that part of the world is a fascinating study that provides useful lessons for the challenges we face today.

Jehovah's Witnesses

The Witnesses, the door-to-door salesmen of Christianity, are what might be called a fanatical eschatological sect, a doomsday cult. They believe that Armageddon is just around the corner, so they have no time for passive associate members. Everyone is expected to hit the streets and proselytize.

The Witnesses believe that Jesus was an enlightened, exalted being, but they reject many mainstream Christian concepts like the Holy Trinity, Hell, the bodily resurrection and divinity of Jesus, and the immortality of the soul. They have a truly epic list of forbidden or deeply discouraged items and practices that includes not just gambling, tobacco, and alcohol but also blood transfusions, flag saluting, military service, voting, lodges, the United Nations, the YMCA, the women's rights movement, Christmas trees, Mother's Day, movies, and higher education. Homosexuality, needless to say, is verboten. They have a history of frequent court battles and, owing to the assistance of the ACLU (whom they nonetheless branded an agent of the devil), an impressive portfolio of US Supreme Court victories. The Witnesses are both up in your face* and way, way out there and easily rate a **high** Sanctimometer© rating.

*One day when I was rushing to get dressed and expecting a friend's momentary arrival, I stumbled onto the best technique for shooing away Jehovah's Witnesses by accidentally greeting them in my underwear. I now simply remove most of my clothing before opening the door, and they leave immediately even when begged not to.

Christian Scientists

Founded by an elderly widow named Mary Baker Eddy during the mid-nineteenth century, this healing cult reveres the wisdom of Jesus and the Bible but rejects most Christian concepts, for example the resurrection and divinity of Jesus, the Holy Trinity, original sin, the devil, heaven, and hell. It is more concerned with Eddy's teachings, which deny the reality of illness and death, and substitute a special form of prayer in place of modern medicine. Her techniques are described in her book *Science and Health With Key to the Scriptures,* about which the author Mark Twain once said, "Of all the strange and frantic and incomprehensible and uninterpretable books which the imagination of man has created, surely this one is the prize sample."

The Church is notable for having a woman founder, for its surprising number of famous and powerful members, and for frequently landing in court due to members denying their children standard medical treatment. Notwithstanding its laudable sponsorship of the journalistically excellent *Christian Science Monitor*, the willingness of Christian Scientists to let their sick children pointlessly die of treatable illnesses earns the church a **high** Sanctimometer© rating.

Unitarian Universalist

This is a creedless church rooted in Christianity. Its gradual disassembly of orthodox Christianity began early in its history, with its rejection of eternal damnation as something unbefitting of God, followed by its rejection of the concept of the Holy Trinity, followed by the falling away of one doctrine after another, to the present day when its seven remaining official guiding principles would function fairly well for the religious right as the very definition of the dreaded secular humanism. Those seven principles are:

1) the inherent dignity of all,

2) justice/equity/compassion,

3) acceptance/encouragement to spiritual growth,

4) the free and responsible search for truth,

5) the right of conscience and use of democratic process,

6) the goal of world community with peace/liberty/justice for all, and

7) respect for the interdependent web of existence.

Although utterly harmless and quite admirable on many levels, The Unitarian/Universalist Church is, on the oceans of world religion, a ship with no anchor, as it honors belief in all its myriad forms. In the pews of its churches one might find an agnostic seated next to a disaffected Jew, a Wiccan, and a Native American spiritualist. They simply take everybody, no questions asked.

The Unitarian Church was the first in America to officially oppose slavery and the first to ordain women for the ministry. It worked early on to reform the nation's prison system, and it has long opposed capital punishment. Its positions on the political issues of the day are predictably very liberal. Oddly, while millions upon millions of people privately hold what are essentially Unitarian/Universalist views, these "spiritual but not religious" Americans remain totally unaware of their natural alignment with this quirky faith.

It would be easy to dismiss Unitarians as a mere blip on the radar screen but for the wildly disproportionate impact its followers have had on society. A small sampling of the many famous Unitarian/Universalists includes Louisa May Alcott, Alexander Graham Bell, William Cullen Bryant, Ralph Waldo Emerson, Oliver Wendell Holmes, Henry Wadsworth Longfellow, and Frank Lloyd Wright. *Moving on to people with only two names*, we see also Susan B. Anthony, P.T. Barnum, Bela Bartok, Clara Barton, Ray Bradbury, e.e. cummings, Charles Dickens, Nathaniel Hawthorne, Linus Pauling, Christopher Reeve, Paul Revere, Albert Schweitzer, Rod Serling, Adlai Stevenson, Daniel Webster, and to complete the evil secular humanist connection, no less than Charles Darwin himself. At least four former U.S. presidents were Unitarians— John Adams, Millard Fillmore, and yes, the triply named John Quincy Adams and William Howard Taft. A fifth, Thomas Jefferson, claimed he would've attended a Unitarian church had there been one near him, and once feebly predicted in a June 26, 1822 letter to Dr. Benjamin Waterhouse that "there is not a young man living in the United States that will not die a Unitarian." The Unitarians, as you can plainly see, are a highly educated bunch, liberal almost to the point of total disintegration, and easily entitled to the lowest of **low** Sanctimometer© ratings.

Mormons

If there were a Billboard Top 40 chart for religions, Mormonism would not be number one, but it would certainly have a bullet next to it. It is growing like a well-watered weed, and if you accept that religions are subject to the same natural selection forces as creatures in nature, you'd have to say Mormonism has the survival traits to thrive in the coming decades and centuries. It is insular (which inhibits corruption by outside influences), it has unifying forced service (the two year mandatory mission), and it is absurdly wealthy (it enforces a literal ten percent tithe).

Yes, the membership of the Church of Jesus Christ of Latter Day Saints, as it prefers to be called, is wildly successful and productive, to be sure. Still the question arises: How impressive is that really when one considers that the Mormon Church to this day strictly prohibits alcohol consumption? The rest of us could build spaceships in our garages and fly to the moon out of our backyards if we gave up drinking. But what would be the point if we had to celebrate our achievements with ice cream cones? I digress.

Mormons consider themselves Christians, although many traditional Christians might disagree. I will make no attempt to summarize or lampoon the lugubrious Book of Mormon here, since the job was already brilliantly done in Mark Twain's *Roughing It*, and it is the sheerest vanity to follow anywhere that man has already trod. Suffice it to say that Mormons believe a whole raft of things that would seem comical or spooky to a mainstream Christian, including the notion that Jesus came to the Western Hemisphere after his crucifixion and resurrection and founded a church among the Native Americans. Then there is that magical underwear...

I will, however, echo a few of Twain's conclusions about the Mormons. As a group they seem harmless enough, and the hateful, murderous treatment they received during their formative years is an atrocious stain on the concept of American freedom of religion. The uncommonly modest demeanor of most Mormons certainly stands out among Christian sects, but one seriously wonders if this is heartfelt or a kind of stealth strategy to camouflage their cult's gradual takeover of the entire planet. Either way, Mormons unfortunately do have, in addition to their well-known past propensity for polygamy, an inescapable history of racism and sexism, some of it quite recent, and their intolerance for homosexuality is unsurpassed among official church dogmas. For this, they really must be given a **high** Sanctimometer© crazy rating. Sorry, Mormons.

***

Now it's time for us to move away from Christianity to the other major players on the world stage. Why? Because maintaining the moral high ground during clashes with Christian Fundamentalists means rising above the ignorance and insularity that underlies their often ignoble endeavors. We must do better!

With that in mind, here are brief summaries of the other prominent faiths or religious groups found around the world.

Judaism

Despite the efforts of ancient Rome and twentieth century Germany to make it a reality, a world without Jews is difficult to imagine. Anyone who doubts this ought to read Thomas Cahill's book on the jaw-dropping achievements of this small Semitic tribe, *The Gifts of the Jews*, or consider the disproportionate impact on the human race of titanic Jewish figures such as Karl Marx, Sigmund Freud, and Albert Einstein. Likewise, the Jewish prophets Abraham, Moses, and

Jesus of Nazareth, through their connections to both Christianity and Islam, are central figures in the religions of more than half the world's population. And it bears mentioning that the Jewish nation of Israel is arguably the world's most likely tinder box for nuclear holocaust. Judaism, for a small religion (0.2 percent of the world's population), is a big deal.

The details of the faith are fairly simple. As described in part one of the book, Judaism honors a covenant made between Abraham, as the representative of the Jewish ethnic group, and God (or Yahweh). Under this covenant the Jews would enjoy the status of God's chosen race if they observed a strict code of conduct. These rules, found in the Torah, the Talmud, and other sacred texts, famously include observance of the Sabbath and circumcision of the foreskin of the penis. There are many dietary restrictions and other prohibitions. Jews must also observe a religious calendar featuring numerous holidays.

Judaism has traditionally discouraged speculation on the afterlife and the immortality of the soul. It specifically rejects the Christian concepts of original sin, salvation, and damnation. It is more concerned with a right relation to God during one's lifetime. As with seemingly all religions, it has become divided roughly into orthodox, liberal, and moderate sects. Remarkably, close to one-fifth of all Jews on the entire planet reside in or around the New York City area.

Islam

The world's second-largest religion takes its name from a word meaning "to submit," as in to submit to the will of God (whom they call Allah). I have already noted its surprising overlap with Christianity and Judaism in various places above. Islam was founded by the prophet Mohammed around 600 A.D. after the angel Gabriel (there's that overlap again) supposedly came to him and began dictating the Koran, the sacred text of Islam. From its start in the Middle East the new religion quickly swept around the Mediterranean and across North Africa, then jumped the

Straits of Gibraltar to get a brief foothold in Spain, Portugal, and parts of France.

Contrary to modern Western stereotypes which portray the Muslim world as backward and stunted, medieval Islam made important contributions to art, poetry, philosophy, and medicine, and according to historian Jared Diamond, "it invented or elaborated windmills, tidal mills, trigonometry, and lateen sails; it made major advances in metallurgy, mechanical and chemical engineering, and irrigation methods; it adopted paper and gunpowder from China and transmitted them to Europe. In the Middle Ages the flow of technology was overwhelmingly from Islam to Europe, rather than from Europe to Islam as it is today." J. Diamond, *Guns, Germs, and Steel: The Fates of Human Societies*, (New York: Norton, 1999), p. 242. During this same period many European Christians were burning witches, catapulting large stones at one another, and going whole lifetimes without a bath.

Like most faiths, Islam has become fragmented. The two main divisions are the Sunnis and the Shias, who split in an ancient dispute over who should succeed the prophet Mohammed as leader of the faith. The vast majority (eighty-five percent or more) of the world's Muslims are Sunni. Shia majorities in Iraq and especially Iran are notable exceptions to this rule. Like Judaism and Christianity, Islam is a fiercely monotheistic faith, which means that, unlike many other religions, its grumpy male godhead insists there can be no other gods, only *him*. And like Judaism, Islam features many cleanliness rituals. Fairly onerous daily prayer obligations are imposed and every Muslim is expected to make at least one trip during his or her lifetime to a shrine in the Arab holy city of Mecca. Of course there is more to it, such as its peculiar (to non-Muslims) treatment of women, but those are the basics.

As you might already know, many Christians, *especially* belligerent Fundamentalists, like to imagine their religion as the polar opposite of Islam, and this delusion intensified after the September 11th terrorist attacks. But remember that one should never, ever let a clueless Christian get away with implying there is a vast difference between the two faiths. The fact is Christianity and Islam are, compared to the world's other religions, virtual first cousins, and Judaism is the grandfather they have in common. Consider this astonishing passage from an official Vatican II declaration of the Roman Catholic Church, written several decades before that fateful day in September of 2001:

> They [Muslims] adore one God, living and enduring, merciful and all-powerful, Maker of heaven and earth and Speaker to men. They strive to submit wholeheartedly even to His inscrutable decrees, just as did Abraham, with whom the Islamic faith is pleased to associate itself. Though they do not acknowledge Jesus as God, they revere him as a prophet. They also honor Mary, His virgin mother; at times they call on her too with devotion. In addition they await the day of judgment when God will give each man his due after raising him up. Consequently they prize the moral life, and give worship to God especially through prayer, almsgiving, and fasting.

So how about it, Christians, Jews, and Muslims? We're not so different after all. What do you say we all hug it out and try to get along?

Hinduism

The world's oldest and third-largest religion, and the faith of the great twentieth century peace activist Mohandas Gandhi, Hinduism is almost unfathomably complex, even by religious standards. Restricted primarily to the Indian subcontinent, it nonetheless has a billion followers who famously believe in reincarnation, the idea that the soul migrates from one life to the next, and karma, the original statement of the idea that what goes around comes around. One might generally say Hinduism is concerned with escape from this chain of incarnations. Yet it has no single historical founder, nor does it have a single defining creed. It does not worship any single god. Paradoxically to Westerners, some Hindus even consider themselves atheists. Hinduism exists in a mind-boggling array of forms. It is often described as being less like a religion in the Western sense and more like a broad way of life.

Buddhism

The world's fourth-largest religion began as a heresy of sorts within Hinduism. Buddhists venerate an Indian sage named Siddhartha Gautama (born in approximately the sixth century B.C.) who came to be known as the Buddha, meaning "the enlightened (or awakened) one." According to Buddhist lore, he was a child of extreme privilege, sheltered from all unpleasantness, who was shocked into his spiritual journey after first witnessing pain, illness, age, and death when he was a teenager. He experimented with various forms of asceticism before an extended meditation under the Bodhi Tree led to his discovery of the "middle way" path between extreme self-indulgence and extreme self-denial.

Buddhism teaches that escape from suffering is achieved through elimination of the three main desires: for pleasure, for prosperity, and for continued existence. This is accomplished by following Buddhist principles such as the eightfold path. A successful Buddhist ultimately achieves Nirvana, the extinction of all desire, hatred, and ignorance. The details vary, and Buddhism is fractured into a wide variety of subgroups, like most religions. In the West it is often followed more like a school of philosophy or psychology than like a religion. As a practical matter, it might be said to blur the lines between them.

Baha'i

Founded by a nineteenth century Persian visionary under a theme of world unity, the Baha'i faith officially advocates the elimination of all forms of prejudice, full equality between the sexes, recognition of the essential oneness of the world's great religions, the elimination of the extremes of poverty and wealth, universal education, the harmony of science and religion, a sustainable balance between nature and technology, and the establishment of a world federal system based on security and the oneness of humanity. In other words, it appears to be the one religion in the world that actually *could* serve as the basis for a decent system of government, but sadly its membership is encouraged to shun politics. That sort of figures, no?

A former leader of the Baha'i church, Shoghi Effendi, once explained it like this:

> [We believe] that religious truth is not absolute but relative, that Divine revelation is a continuous and progressive process, that all the great religions of the world are divine in origin, that their basic principles are in complete harmony, that their aims and purposes are one and the same, that their teachings are but facets of one truth, that their functions are complementary, that they differ only in the nonessential aspects of their doctrines, and that their missions represent successive stages in the spiritual evolution of human society. (Shoghi Effendi, "The Faith of Baha'u'llah," in *World Order*, Vol. 7, No. 2 1972-73, p.7)

One might say Baha'i resembles Unitarianism in its tolerance of a broad range of beliefs and its peaceful goals. But as an institution, it is not immune from problems; its writings are dense and nearly impenetrable, and it continues to give off a mystical Persian aroma. Still, it deserves credit for official guiding principles of rare progressive quality among the world's religions. Let's all be extra nice to the Baha'i.

Sikhism

Like Hinduism and Buddhism, this is a very large world religion that originated on the Indian subcontinent. Refreshingly simple in its ideology, Sikhism teaches that there is one god who is beyond human definition and who requires no particular ritual worship. Sikhs are expected to love and meditate on God and live moral and peaceful lives while shunning lust, anger, greed, emotional attachment, and ego. Sikhism encourages charity and forbids discrimination, which ought to embarrass the rest of us considering Sikhs are often harassed and even assaulted in the United States simply because they wear turbans. Neither Arab nor Muslim, Sikhs have nonetheless been the victims of hundreds of misguided hate crimes since September 11th, including the ghastly 2012 murder of six members at a Sikh temple in Oak Creek, Wisconsin. So let's be extra nice to them, too.

Shintoism

Shintoism refers to the traditional religious practices of the Japanese people, which are intended to keep them spiritually linked to their ancestors and to their culture's distant past. Like Hinduism, it can appear to Westerners to be more like a lifestyle or a set of customs than a religion. Many of its practitioners also utilize Buddhist rituals but consider this overlap unremarkable.

Jainism

Yet another religion from India with Hindu influences, Jainism is among the oldest faiths in the world. Despite its surprising choice of a swastika for its official symbol, it is a peaceful faith devoted to the elimination of violence through the mastery of self-control. The universe and the soul are considered eternal, without beginning or end. Jains emphasize the importance of individual perspective and reject the concept of absolute truth. To illustrate the point, they provided the world with the familiar story of blind men describing an elephant based only on the parts they could individually touch. Jains fittingly encourage broad tolerance of opposing viewpoints and outside religions.

Jain ascetics are so committed to extreme nonviolence that they wear gauze masks over their mouths to guard against accidentally inhaling insects. When they walk, they likewise sweep the ground ahead of them for the protection of crawling insects. For fear of harming aquatic insect larvae, they stay indoors during rainy season. That is the only time of year they aren't wandering barefoot and literally naked, accepting only modest gifts of vegetarian food. Kudos to you, Jain monks—that's dedication! But don't try that around here or you'll soon find yourself clothed in an orange jumpsuit.

The symbol of Jainism.

Chinese Religions

As with Hinduism, Chinese religious practices don't fit neatly into Western categories. The Chinese do not have a single predominant faith, and their religious traditions might again look to Westerners more like a set of cultural customs than a belief system. Of course, China's communist government is officially atheist, but the Chinese people are in fact fairly religious, and given that there are going on two billion of them, they and their diverse beliefs at least ought to be recognized.

In addition to Christianity, Islam, and Buddhism, a variety of ethnic religious traditions can be found in modern China, including Confucianism, Taoism, and various folk religions. They tend to be polytheistic (nonexclusive), and often emphasize ethical conduct and the veneration of ancestors, among other principles.

***

There are, of course, many other world religions, some of them fairly large and most of them well developed. Christians, however, insist on maintaining their custom of assuming that all non-Christians are dangerous heathens, pagans, or devil worshipers. Of course this is ludicrous. Human beings in every part of the world have long-standing belief systems of some type* with the vast majority of them featuring an ethical component. Not only that, they all have a lot of catching up to do to match the destruction wrought by the so-called great religions, as you are about to learn.

*Some researchers theorize that a human propensity for agency detection, for sensing the work of a divine hidden hand, serves an evolutionary purpose. This theory could also serve as the very definition of irony.

PART FOUR

KNOW THE CHRISTIAN ABUSES

OK, brace yourself. What follows is a list, nowhere near exhaustive, naming some of the worst abuses of Christianity and the Bible throughout history. Any Fundamentalist brash enough to invade your personal space with his unsolicited message at least ought to be challenged to atone for these disgraceful episodes. Looking at the list below, one could make the argument that no other phenomenon in human history has ever proven so harmful.

Let me give you a few examples. Isolation of the anthrax virus? Not as harmful, humans have for the most part managed to keep it safely stored in secure laboratories. Invention of the nuclear bomb? Not as harmful, it resulted in a one-time kill of a quarter of a million people. Texting and driving? Not as harmful, only eleven teen deaths per day on average. In contrast, behold the Christian legacy:

To Justify Slavery

That the Bible played a significant role in one of history's worst crimes against humanity should not surprise us. What *is* a bit surprising is that, unlike most hateful Christian undertakings, it was *not* accomplished solely by reference to the hard-hearted Christian Old Testament. Consider these quotations from the New Testament:

> Servants, be obedient to them that are your masters according to the flesh, with fear and trembling, in singleness of your heart, as unto Christ. (Ephesians 6:5)

> Servants, be subject to your masters with all fear; not only
> to the good and gentle, but also to the forward. For this is
> thankworthy, if a man for conscience toward God endure
> grief, suffering wrongfully. For what glory is it, if, when ye
> be buffeted for your faults, ye shall take it patiently? But if,
> when ye do well, and suffer for it, ye take it patiently, this
> is acceptable with God. For even hereunto were ye called:
> because Christ also suffered for us, leaving us an example,
> that ye should follow his steps. (1 Peter 2:18-21)

As one might guess from these depressing passages that equate being a good slave with being a good Christian, the Bible unfortunately contains no explicit prohibition against slavery. And so it was that for hundreds of years, Christian slave owners actually felt encouraged by their own religion in their greedy reliance on "the peculiar institution." Take for example this excerpt from "A Scriptural View," an influential pamphlet written and circulated by Baptist reverend Thorton Stringfellow of Virginia before the US Civil War:

> ...Jesus Christ recognized this institution as one that was
> lawful among men, and regulated its relative duties...I
> affirm then, first (and no man denies) that Jesus Christ
> has not abolished slavery by a prohibitory command...

So if you are one of those who regard Christianity as a useless charade, you really need look no further than its antebellum role in justifying slavery to see that it certainly does have its uses. And it is no secret that Southern plantation owners in the United States went even further and effectively used Christian instruction of their slaves as a form of behavior modification. When you consider that slave masters also steered the mating activity of slaves to produce sturdier stock, you come face to face with this soul-crushing realization: for two and a half centuries—from 1619, when the first slaves were brought to Virginia, until the 1865 passage of the Thirteenth Amendment—millions upon millions of African captives in this country were the unwilling subjects of a depraved psycho-biological experiment in which they were bred and conditioned for certain physical traits and temperament, exactly like dogs. *Like dogs.*

However, in a sweet irony suggesting the existence of a benevolent God, it was exactly such a person—a strong but gentle black man who refused every provocation to violence—that emerged as the triumphant leader of the civil rights movement of the 1960s: the Rev. Dr. Martin Luther King, Jr. Can I get an "amen?"

This ability of Christians to harmonize slavery with the Golden Rule of Luke 6:31, wherein Jesus commanded his followers to "do unto others as you would have them do unto you," is a stark tribute to their breathtaking capacity for holding mutually exclusive beliefs simultaneously.

Eventually, however, they figured it out, albeit at the end of a Union musket barrel. No Christian today could possibly reconcile his or her faith with the literal ownership of another human being. But as we have seen with various other discontinued biblical practices, such as polygamy and animal sacrifice, Christians transitioned very quietly from their Bibles to doing the right thing, and shook off the whole experience like a bad dream, not bothering to remember what happened so as not to repeat it. And while we can be grateful that they took this step, we are left to wonder why each time Christians depart from the antiquated moral code of their Bible in service of a higher truth, they act as if they are doing so for the very first time.

To Support Claims of the Superiority of Whites

In this country, the notorious Ku Klux Klan provides the most conspicuous example of the Bible and Christian imagery being used to support claims of white supremacy. Formed in 1866, the year after the passage of the Thirteenth Amendment and the end of the US Civil War, the KKK boasted a membership of roughly two million Klansmen in its heyday of the 1920s. Its ceremonies typically featured an altar with a Christian Bible laid open to Romans chapter twelve—a testament to how utterly stupid KKK members were, as this passage's plain language would lead any half-sensible person to an interpretation diametrically opposite that of the Klan—along with a cross, an American flag, and a sword representative of the fight against the supposed enemies of Christianity.

The Klan recruited openly in America's churches, gaining members not only from Christian laity, but from clergy. Their official anthem was a dreary dirge of their own concoction called "The Fiery Cross," but their ceremonies also featured mainstream Christian hymns like "Onward Christian Soldiers" and "The Old Rugged Cross." The prayers with which they opened and closed their meetings included the phrase "the living Christ is a Klansman's criterion of character!"

Sadly for Christianity, it is beyond reasonable dispute that it has provided moral cover for a number of white supremacy movements throughout history, the KKK prominent among them, and it continues to do so to this day. And did I mention that Adolph Hitler was raised a Catholic? That's a fact, Jack.

To Support Claims of the Inferiority of Blacks

It is known as the Curse of Ham (or sometimes the Sin of Ham or Curse of Canaan). I am talking about the muddled Old Testament tale of possible incest involving Noah, of ark-building fame, and his son, Ham, a tale that for many centuries was used to justify the maltreatment and enslavement of dark-skinned peoples. The biblical passage in its entirety reads as follows:

> Noah was the first tiller of the soil. He planted a vineyard; and he drank of the wine, and became drunk, and lay uncovered in his tent. And Ham, the father of Canaan, saw the nakedness of his father, and told his two brothers

outside. Then Shem and Japheth took a garment, laid it on their shoulders, and walked backward and covered the nakedness of their father; their faces were turned away, and they did not see their father's nakedness. When Noah awoke from his wine and knew what his youngest son had done to him, he said "Cursed be Canaan [Ham's son]; a slave of slaves shall he be to his brothers." He also said "Blessed by the Lord my God be Shem; and let Canaan be his slave. God enlarge Japheth, and let him dwell in the tents of Shem; and let Canaan be his slave." (Genesis 9:20-27)

Bear in mind that, while the passage speaks of merely seeing nakedness, we have already observed examples from the Bible of how "knowing" a person could mean having sex with him or her. Similarly, some scholars speculate that "seeing" Noah's nakedness here might insinuate some kind of sex act between Noah and Ham, or Noah and his grandson, Canaan, at Ham's direction. Note that it speaks of "what his youngest son had *done to him*" (emphasis added). Eww.

A couple of things really need to be said at this point. First, *I warned you* that the book of Genesis was a filthy, dirty thing. And second, how in the *hell* did white Christians distill a justification for slavery out of *that*? Did you read even one word about skin color in that entire paragraph?

The passage identifies Ham as the brother of Shem and Japheth. How is he supposed to be black and they white? Although polygamy is common in the Old Testament, the book of Genesis consistently refers to Noah's wife in the singular. Nevertheless, white slave owners for many centuries pointed to this story as their justification for enslaving captured Africans, claiming through a convoluted and self-serving genealogical argument that as descendants of Ham and Canaan such people deserved to be exploited. Well, we have already investigated the reliability of biblical genealogies, have we not? Bear in mind too that this chapter closes with the preposterous assertion that Noah thereafter lived to the overripe age of 950 years.

Despite its illogic, the myth that Ham's Curse took the form of darkened skin persisted until the nineteenth century, when Confederate slaveholders were still utilizing it, as evidenced by author and slavery opponent Hinton Rowan Helper* writing in 1860 that slave owners "bandy among themselves, in traditional order, certain garbled passages of Scripture, such, for instance, as that concerning poor old besotted Noah's intemperate curse of Ham, which...they regard, or pretend to regard, as investing them with full and perfect license to practice [slavery]."

Regarding this unforgiveable perversion of the Bible, the Rev. Dr. Martin Luther King, Jr. remarked: "The greatest blasphemy of the whole ugly process was that the white man ended up making God his partner in the exploitation of the Negro." Well said, good doctor.

*Helper was the author of an influential book opposing slavery, *The Impending Crisis of the South* (1857), which argued that slave ownership contributed to the economic inferiority of the American South. He later served as a foreign diplomat in the Lincoln Administration. He was nonetheless a virulent racist.

To Persecute Jews

> [Roman governor Pontius] Pilate said to them, "Then what shall I do with Jesus who is called Christ?" They [the Jews] all said, "Let him be crucified." And he said, "Why? What evil has he done?" But they shouted all the more, "Let him be crucified."

> So when Pilate saw that he was gaining nothing, but rather that a riot was beginning, he took water and washed his hands before the crowd, saying, "I am innocent of this man's blood; see to it yourselves." And all the people answered, "His blood be on us and on our children!" (Matthew 27:22-25)

And so began two thousand years of Christians illogically blaming the Jews for the death of Jesus of Nazareth, a Jew, despite the fact that their Christian religion is based precisely on the necessity of his death for their salvation. I know, it's crazy.

Anti-Semitism is an immense historical subject that could fill many, many volumes, and people who doubt its existence really need look no further than the Nazi Holocaust of the twentieth century, when Hitler's regime in Germany ruthlessly exterminated six million Jews like so many cockroaches. It is enough for our purposes to make several key points about that history insofar as it relates to Christianity.

The first is that there is certainly no shortage of biblical authority for anti-Semitism. In addition to the above passage from Matthew, there is the following vitriol from Saint Stephen to the high priest in Jerusalem:

> Ye stiffnecked and uncircumcised in heart and ears, ye do always resist the Holy Ghost: as your fathers did, so do ye. Which of the prophets have not your fathers persecuted? And they have slain them which shewed before the coming of the Just One: of whom ye have been now the betrayers and murderers. (Acts 7:51-52)

So it was never difficult for Christians to find biblical authority for their hatred of the Jews. Not that they ever needed much.

There was also ample historical "evidence" of God's willingness to punish the Jews. Throughout the first Christian millennium it was widely believed that the Roman destruction of Jerusalem and its Temple in 70 A.D. and the subsequent Jewish Diaspora were the race's punishment for killing Jesus. During medieval times various slanderous myths about Jews arose, including the notorious blood libel, a persistent European rumor that Jews used the blood of murdered Christian children as sacramental wine in their Passover ritual (never mind that Jewish Law strictly prohibited any use of any blood whatsoever).

247

Then, by quirk of fate, the role of money lender fell to Jews when the Catholic Church in the twelfth century forbade its members to charge interest to borrowers based on the authority of the Old Testament (Exodus 22:25 and Deuteronomy 23:19). This development perhaps as much as any other produced chronic European resentment of the Jews that persisted all the way to the rise of the German Third Reich* under Nazism.

Unbelievably, anti-Semitism somehow survived the Nazi Holocaust in Germany. It was not until 1961 that the World Council of Churches finally condemned it as incompatible with the teachings of Jesus, and only in 1962 did the Second Vatican Council finally remove the phrase "perfidious [i.e. deceitful, conniving] Jews" from the Catholic Good Friday worship liturgy. The Vatican did not officially recognize and mourn the Jewish Holocaust until April 1994, nearly fifty years after the fact.

Modern-day Protestants are no less enthusiastic about bashing the race that produced their Lord and savior, Jesus Christ. Take a look at this excerpt from an editorial in the July/August 1991 issue of Pat Robertson's Christian Coalition newsletter:

> The New Testament reveals that Jews "both killed the Lord Jesus and their own prophets, and have persecuted us; and they please not God, and are contrary to all men" (1 Thessalonians 2:15). History records the terrible sufferings the Jewish people have experienced as a result.

But here's the thing: history likewise records that these sufferings were, in large part, meted out not by God but by Christians acting hatefully in God's name. For shame, Christianity, for shame.

*Long before Hitler, an aging and perhaps somewhat senile Martin Luther set a shameful example for sixteenth century Germany by publicly condemning the "damned, rejected race of Jews" in his mind-numbing treatise "On the Jews and Their Lies," published in 1543. In it he referred to them as "venomous, bitter, vindictive, tricky serpents, assassins, and children of the devil," and called for their synagogues to be burned and their houses destroyed, and for them to be put in stables, "like gypsies." He closed his diatribe like this: "To sum up, dear princes and nobles who have Jews in your domains, if this advice of mine does not suit you, then find a better one so that you and we may be free of this insufferable devilish burden—the Jews." Ouch.

To Subordinate Women

It is not the least bit difficult to find support in the Bible for the domestic and social subordination of women so familiar to Christian tradition. The Bible is littered with verses directly on point.

> Wives, submit yourselves unto your own husbands, as unto the Lord. For the husband is the head of the wife, even as Christ is the head of the church: and he is the savior of the body. Therefore as the church is subject unto Christ, so let the wives be to their own husbands in every thing. (Ephesians 5:22-24)

> But I would have you know, that the head of every man is Christ; and the head of the woman is the man; and the head of Christ is God. (1 Corinthians 11:3)

> For the man is not of the woman; but the woman of the man. Neither was the man created for the woman; but the woman for the man. (1 Corinthians 11:8-9)*

*According to blues legend B.B. King, however, this states it backwards. Women are God's greatest creation, he claimed, and men are God's gift to them.

The subordination of women starts very early in the Bible, where the book of Genesis blames a woman for the fall of mankind in the Garden of Eden, for which all women received as punishment the "sorrow" of motherhood.

> Unto the woman he said, I will greatly multiply thy sorrow and thy conception; in sorrow thou shalt bring forth children; and thy desire shall be to thy husband, and he shall rule over thee. (Genesis 3:16)

This sorrow came to be associated with "the curse" of women's menstruation, the frequent subject of derogatory Old Testament commentary (see also Genesis 31:35, Leviticus 12:2-5, Leviticus 15:19-30, Leviticus 18:19). And while several women appear as heroines in the Old Testament, such as the prophetesses Miriam and Deborah, they stand as rare exceptions to the rule of male preeminence under Jewish Law. Likewise, although the Old Testament book of Ruth features a female protagonist and provides the oft-heard poetic tribute to female friendship "whither thou goest, I will go," in the end it is just another disturbing example of the Hebrew obsession with patrilineal succession in the ownership of lands.

The New Testament is no less misogynistic in its rhetoric, but it is hard not to notice the changing role of women. So you find an abundance of quotes like this:

> But I suffer not a woman to teach, nor to usurp authority over the man, but to be in silence. For Adam was first formed, then Eve. And Adam was not deceived, but the woman being deceived was in the transgression. (I Tim 2:12-14)

And yet, you also see Jesus interacting freely and respectfully with women. And you can read between the lines to see prominent roles being played by the women close to him in all four of the gospels. Not only that but you see women serving as early church leaders after Jesus's death, such as the deaconess Phoebe, Saint Paul's assistant and his formal emissary to Rome. Sadly this meant nothing to the Christian men who used the Bible to perpetuate subservient roles for women right up to the twentieth century.

Among the many women who fought back against this Bible-based subjugation over the years, suffragette Elizabeth Cady Stanton of Johnstown, New York stood out. She co-authored *The Woman's Bible*, published in two parts in 1895 and 1898, which rewrote much of the Christian Bible from a female perspective as a rebuttal to traditional biblical arguments against women's rights. Although the book, a best seller, was widely criticized, with some calling it the work of Satan, it provided useful ammunition not just for the women's suffrage movement, but also for those later advocating passage of the Equal Rights Amendment and the ordination of women ministers (discussed below).

A colorful character, Stanton once responded like this to a wealthy woman who was reluctant to contribute to a women's college because her minister told her there was nothing in the Bible to support it:

> Tell him he is mistaken. If he will turn to 2 Chronicles 34:22, he will find that when Josiah, the king, sent the wise men to consult Huldah, the prophetess, about the book of laws...they found Huldah in the college in Jerusalem, thoroughly well informed on questions of state, while Shallum, her husband, was keeper of the robes. I suppose his business was to sew on the royal buttons.

From this you can see she was a pioneer in fighting off Fundamentalist yokels with cold, hard facts and a quick wit, for which we honor and salute her. Elizabeth Cady Stanton died in 1902, eighteen years before U.S. women were finally given the right to vote that she worked so hard to win.

To Accuse Unconventional Women of Witchcraft

Thou shalt not suffer a witch to live. (Exodus 22:18)

A man or a woman that hath a familiar spirit, or that is a wizard, shall surely be put to death: they shall stone them with stones: their blood shall be upon them. (Leviticus 20:27)

Although belief in the occult has been around forever, the heyday of European interest in witchcraft occurred during the Late Middle Ages and Early Modern Period. In all, the era of Christian witch hunts only lasted about 250 years, but it took a grisly toll.

The Catholic Church's heightened interest in witchcraft began in the fifteenth century with the Spanish Inquisition, the Spanish Crown's attempt to restore Catholic orthodoxy to the kingdom following a period of Muslim rule on the Iberian Peninsula (yes, that really happened). Adding to this was the publication of the *Malleus Maleficarum* (*Hammer of the Witches*), written by Catholic clergyman Heinrich Kramer in 1486 as a rebuttal to those in the Church claiming witchcraft did not exist. Known in Kramer's native German as *Der Hexenhammer* (awesome name!), the tract was a guide to the effective identification and prosecution of witches.

Then, in 1611, when James the First of England, who was known for his fascination with the occult, produced his King James Version of the Bible, it utilized terms like *witch* and *wizard* in a number of places where the Hebrew and Greek words had previously been translated in other ways, such as *sorcerer* or *diviner.*

All of these factors, as well as official encouragement from Pope Innocent VIII (see the entry on him in part five, below), created an environment that proved very dangerous to female social outliers. The primary targets were unmarried women, midwives, women business owners, women who lived "in sin" with men, and women who challenged male authority. During this witch hunt era, some historians estimate, as many as one hundred thousand people were put to death for the "crime" of practicing witchcraft.

A few techniques of the witch hunters remain well known to this day, such as throwing the accused into deep water to see if she lived (guilty, burn her) or died (innocent, give her a Christian burial). It was also common to strip the accused to search for irregular features like extra nipples, even a wart or a birthmark might do. The problem, of course, was that these trials contained no procedural safeguards, so the burden of proof was on the accused to prove she was not a witch—not an easy thing to do at the time for let's say a smart, strong-willed, independent midwife with the audacity to advise fellow women on reproductive health and look men unapologetically in the eye.

It's hard to digest what so often happened next, but it's not hard to imagine.

On this side of the Atlantic, the notorious Salem witch trials in Massachusetts colony during the late seventeenth century provide a vivid illustration of the mass hysteria that so often surrounded these accusations of witchcraft. More than two hundred colonists, most of them women, were accused of witchcraft. Twenty were found guilty and executed based on coerced testimony, much of it from children—nineteen by hanging, and one by *peine forte et dure*, in which the accused is gradually pressed to death by stacked weights.

This Christian tendency to accuse strong women of witchcraft has not died out completely in this country. Three centuries after Salem, we still see the impulse in this quote from a 1992 fundraising letter by televangelist Pat Robertson in opposition to a proposed state Equal Rights Amendment:

> The feminist agenda is not about equal rights for women...
> It is about a socialist, anti-family political movement that
> encourages women to leave their husbands, kill their

children, practice witchcraft, destroy capitalism, and become Lesbians.

Nice work, Pat. Pope Innocent VIII would no doubt be proud.

To Oppose the Ordination of Women as Priests

> Let your women keep silence in the churches: for it is not permitted unto them to speak; but they are commanded to be under obedience, as also saith the law. And if they will learn any thing, let them ask their husbands at home: for it is a shame for women to speak in the church. (1 Corinthians 14:34-35)

For two thousand years the leadership of the Christian Church has been a men's club. From the earliest days of Christianity until the mid-twentieth century, women were denied meaningful roles in officiating worship services or administering church affairs on all but the lowest of levels. This was based primarily on hare-brained biblical rants such as the one above, many of them from the pen of Saint Paul. This is both a pity and a historical mystery, since it is also clear from those Pauline letters that he placed great trust in a number of important women during the formative years of the Church, including the early deaconess Phoebe, mentioned above, and Priscilla, who played a vital role in the establishment of the nascent church in Rome along with her husband, Aquila.

Thankfully most (but not all) Protestant Churches have been ordaining women into their clergy for decades now and are much the better for it, but the Catholic and Eastern Orthodox Churches remain firmly opposed. This is based on ancient bureaucratic church decrees prohibiting it, plus the sentiment that since Jesus selected no women apostles it simply wasn't meant to be.

This is the reasoning of a child. If a lack of historical precedent were a good enough reason to exclude women from a vocation, we wouldn't

have female judges, doctors, scientists, politicians, athletes, police offi-
cers, firefighters, soldiers, or the countless other invaluable women pro-
fessionals who serve so ably. The world would be greatly impoverished.

These churches still are.

To Define and Punish Sodomy as a Crime

American criminal codes that once made sodomy illegal in all fifty
of the United States were understandably vague. The vast majority of
them were to some degree based directly on the biblical prohibition
against sodomy, which was likewise vague. The reason for this is as comical as it is tragic: the authors of both lacked the courage to describe the
offense specifically, and so it went by pseudonyms such as "the unspeakable act" or "the detestable and abominable vice." Yet it was a crime, in
some cases punishable by death.

What is sodomy? It remains hard to define, but most sources agree
that it includes any non-procreative sex act. It takes its name from the
story of a righteous Jew named Lot, found in chapter nineteen of the
Old Testament book of Genesis. Lot lived in the notoriously lustful city
of Sodom (neighbor of the almost equally infamous Gomorrah). The
iconic Jewish figure Abraham lived nearby, and being on a first-name
basis with Yahweh, he learned that the two cities were marked for destruction on account of their evil ways.

The ensuing conversation between Abraham and Yahweh would
make a great vaudeville comedy sketch, though it might attract the ire of
the Anti-Defamation League. The two engaged in a bargaining session
that set the tone for four thousand years of Jewish stereotyping, with
Yahweh first agreeing to spare the cities if fifty righteous people lived
there. Abraham haggled it down to forty-five, then to forty, then thirty,
then twenty, then ten.

Ultimately it wasn't enough, and fire and brimstone supposedly
rained down on both cities, destroying them completely. But first a kinky
episode took place in which two angels came to visit Lot in his home and

were set upon by randy locals who wanted to "know" them. Lot's solution? He offered the unruly crowd his two virgin daughters instead, to do with as they pleased. Fortunately for the girls, the mob declined his proposal of heterosexual gang rape.

Lacking the requisite number of righteous co-residents, Lot and his family were forced to flee. But don't worry; the story has a happy ending, one that set the tone for four millennia of moral justice. *Here goes.* As they fled, Lot's wife looked over her shoulder to watch the pyrotechnics and was turned into a pillar of salt. Then later Lot's two daughters got him drunk in a cave and fornicated with him on consecutive nights, after which both conceived children. The End. I'm not kidding. You can look it up at Genesis 19:24-38.

So this, *this* is the story from which Jews and Christians gleaned the moral authority for four thousand years of criminalizing non-procreative sex acts, often punishing violators with lengthy prison sentences or worse.

The mind reels.

A telling example is the heart-rending story of the 1895 trial and sodomy conviction of the brilliant English writer and pithy wit Oscar Wilde, who, after a hung jury and retrial, received the maximum sentence of two years at hard labor for "gross indecency" even though he'd acted in private with a consenting adult male. The judge pronounced the sentence "totally inadequate for a case such as this," while Wilde's response, "And I? May I say nothing, my Lord?" was drowned out by vicious courtroom jeers and cries of "Shame!"

There will now be a moment of silence while we all grieve...

To this day sodomy remains a serious crime, sometimes punishable by death, in seventy-some countries mainly located in Africa, Asia, and the Middle East. Most of them have Muslim majority populations, so I suppose Christianity can beam with pride that it has fallen to second-place in the faith-based criminalization of sodomy business.

Still, as recently as 1986 the U.S. Supreme Court upheld the constitutionality of sodomy laws in the hilariously-named *Bowers v. Hardwick* decision. But the prohibition finally got soft in its old age, going completely limp sometime after its four-thousandth birthday in the 2003 case of *Lawrence v. Texas* (where else?). By a majority vote of six to three, the court at long last declared criminal sodomy laws unconstitutional. I suppose it was too much to expect a unanimous decision.

To Persecute Homosexuals

Roman emperor Justinian the Great, the Eastern Orthodox patron who reigned from 527 to 565 A.D., was so convinced that the many natural disasters, plagues, and famines afflicting his empire were God's punishment for rampant homosexuality in the realm that his Justinian Code, which rewrote the Roman *Corpus Juris Civilis*, specified in Section 4.18 a penalty of death for "those who dare to indulge their unspeakable lust with males."

Not enough has changed in the fifteen hundred years that followed. As I described above, most developed countries have finally decriminalized homosexuality, but there remain many parts of the world where homosexuals still face severe persecution. The United States has made positive strides since the days when homosexuals such as Matthew Shepard and Harvey Milk were murdered for making straight people feel uncomfortable while the nation mostly shrugged. We can certainly feel good about the landmark marital equality decision by the U.S. Supreme Court in *Obergefell v. Hodges* only twenty years after passage of the retrograde federal Defense of Marriage Act. Yet the U.S. continues to lack broad federal constitutional protection against anti-LGBT discrimination. With polls of American youths showing wide agreement across most demographic divisions in favor of correcting this, it seems the only remaining obstacle to real reform is for everyone currently over the age of about thirty to die and get the hell out of its way.

To their credit, many state and local governments are stepping forward to alleviate the problem. But where there is opposition, such as the legislative efforts to undermine *Obergefell* under the guise of protecting religious freedom, it is a safe bet that it comes from conservative Christian groups and the cynical politicians who pander to them. As described in part three of this book, so-called Christian organizations like the Westboro Baptist Church have long mimicked Justinian the Great, blaming societal tolerance of homosexuality for everything from the September 11th terrorist attacks and AIDS to the ongoing rash of school shootings. And this kind of thinking is unfortunately not limited to the lunatic fringe. In 2004 the Christian U.S. Congresswoman Michele Bachmann (R-MN) reacted to the news of pop singer Melissa Etheridge's cancer diagnosis by telling the conservative education group known as EdWatch "This may be an opportunity for her to be open to some spiritual things, now that she is suffering with that physical disease. She is a lesbian."

To paraphrase Winston Churchill's famous retort to the ugly woman who accused him of being drunk—Yes, Michele, and you are ignorant, but Ms. Etheridge's cancer at least is in remission.

To Prohibit Masturbation

The Christian ban on masturbation has a long history that continues right up to modern Vatican pronouncements. As I mentioned earlier, the Church's formal opposition to non-procreative sex acts is simply absolute, and the *Youth Catechism of the Catholic Church* (or YOUCAT) states unequivocally that:

> Masturbation is an offense against love, because it makes the excitement of sexual pleasure an end in itself and uncouples it from the holistic unfolding of love between a man and a woman. That is why 'sex with yourself' is a contradiction in terms.

Because it appears that as a good Catholic, you aren't allowed to love yourself. Well, considering what you've learned so far in this book, you might just be ready to agree with that notion. But it still doesn't adequately explain this Christian proscription.

The biblical authority condemning masturbation is ostensibly found in the Old Testament story of Onan, after whom the act was long referred to as "onanism" in Christian circles. But here's the thing: Onan never masturbates in the story. This is the entire tale, from start to finish:

> And Er, Judah's firstborn, was wicked in the sight of the Lord; and the Lord slew him. And Judah said unto Onan, Go into thy brother's wife, and marry her, and raise up seed to thy brother. And Onan knew that the seed should not be his; and it came to pass, when he went in unto his brother's wife, that he spilled it on the ground, lest that he should give seed to his brother. And the thing which he did displeased the Lord: wherefore he slew him also. (Genesis 38:7-10)

And that is it, end of story! Did I mention to you that Genesis is a sick, sick book?

So yes, the biblical prohibition against masturbation comes from this peculiar story of Onan, who was too anguished to knock up his grieving, widowed sister-in-law, and committed the unpardonable sin of *coitus interruptus*. And oh, by the way, Yahweh was so unhappy with this outcome that he slew Onan.

Does it make sense? Not one bit, but there it is. In fairness, there are other verses in the Bible suggestive of sexual moderation, which one might arguably extend to regulate auto-eroticism. For example, this exhortation to early Christians by Saint Paul: "Let not sin therefore reign in your mortal body, that ye should obey it in the lusts thereof" (Romans 6:12).

That actually does make a certain amount of sense along the lines of the old proverb about everything in moderation. But remember also this version by our friend Oscar Wilde: "Everything in moderation, including moderation." And for you Catholics, there is also this classic Woody Allen punch-line, which doubles as a rebuttal to the YOUCAT: "Don't knock masturbation—it's sex with someone I love!"

To Justify the Corporal Punishment of Children

Many believe the classic child-rearing adage "spare the rod and spoil the child" comes directly from the Bible. In reality, it is from a satire by British poet Samuel Butler entitled "Hudibras," published in the late seventeenth century. In it a fickle knight tries to woo a widow, who suggests he prove his love with a dramatic suicide attempt. When he understandably balks, she offers him an easier path: he can allow her to whip him. Now dear reader, if you have started getting the impression from my book that we live in the *least* perverted era yet known to human history then I wouldn't blame you, but I swear I'm not making this stuff up.

In any case, the widow goes on to extol the virtues of whipping, closing with this stanza:

> If matrimony and hanging go
> By dest'ny, why not whipping too?
> What med'cine else can cure the fits
> Of lovers when they lose their wits?
> Love is a boy by poets stil'd;
> Then spare the rod and spoil the child.

The good knight Hudibras promises to enroll in a "school of lashing" if the widow will get him released from jail, except he breaks his promise to her after going free. Few commentators believe the author meant to render *parenting advice* of all things, but fate is also fickle, and that's how it turned out.

However, the sad truth is that at least five different verses from the Old Testament book of Proverbs likewise reference the use of a rod for beating children. For example:

He that spareth his rod hateth his son: but he that loveth him chasteneth him betimes. (Proverbs 13:24)

Foolishness is bound up in the heart of a child; but the rod of correction shall drive it far from him. (Proverbs 22:15)

Withhold not correction from the child: for if thou beatest him with the rod, he shall not die. Thou shalt beat him with the rod, and shalt deliver his soul from hell. (Proverbs 23:13-14)

So if caning your offspring is how you like to roll, you will get little resistance from old school Christians, many of whom steadfastly believe in these Old Testament maxims. Nineteen hundred years of unquestioning Christian tolerance for the severe corporal punishment of children stands as proof of that.

Still, one has to wonder what became of the example set by Jesus, when he instructed his followers not to chasten the unruly children flocking to him, telling them to instead "suffer the little children to come unto me" (Mark 10:14).

Poor little Mary Ellen McCormack was the subject of the first known prosecution for child abuse in American jurisprudence, in New York in 1874. If you were born before then, tough luck!

Incredibly, the court was forced to resort to animal cruelty laws to get Mary Ellen removed from her home and her foster mother convicted. Even today, it is thought that three U.S. children die each day from some type of parental mistreatment. (From "Case Shined First Light on Abuse of Children," by Howard Markel, M.D., New York Times, December 14, 2009.)

To Justify Torture

An observer with casual knowledge of Church history might cynically joke that Christianity and torture have always gone together like peanut butter and jelly. But that would be wrong and would give the longevity of the sandwich far too much credit. The first peanut butter and jelly sandwich probably dates back only one hundred years or so, while torture as a Christian institution can be traced to the fifteenth century Spanish Inquisition, if not further, and lasted until the nineteenth century or longer, depending on your definition.

As I've pointed out in other sections of this book, the key role Christian torture played in the Inquisition and the witch hunt era is as undeniable as it is unbefitting. So rather than rehash its sordid history, I'll simply offer these glimpses of some (not nearly all) of the Church's favorite torture devices, and leave the rest to your imagination.

The Judas Cradle: A form of impalement in which the naked offender was lowered onto the point of a wooden pyramid so that it penetrated the anus or vagina. Then he or she was manipulated by ropes to adjust the level of pain.

The heretic's fork: A favorite of the Inquisition, it consisted of a metal fork with sharp tines at both ends fixed in place with a leather strap around the offender's neck, with one pointed end planted in the chest and the other under the chin. The person wearing it would then be restrained in an upright position so that falling asleep caused the fork to gouge the neck and chest, producing excruciating pain.

The lead sprinkler: This fiendish device had the appearance of a holy water sprinkler, but was filled with molten metal (or tar in less serious cases) that was flicked on the perpetrator's exposed flesh.

The pear of anguish (or choke pear): This less-common device was purportedly used, for example, on women who self-aborted pregnancies or on homosexuals. It was designed to be inserted into the vagina of a woman or the anus of a man and slowly spread open until it achieved sufficient internal organ damage.

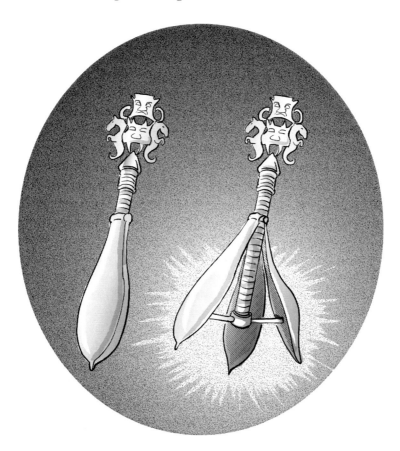

The head crusher: Another favorite of the Inquisition, it was used to extract confessions, though it is hard to see how a heretic could confess with this device slowly compressing his head until his jaw shattered and his eyes burst. Phrases like "turning the screw" and being "screwed" perhaps originate with the use of devices like this.

Burning at the stake: A common technique for disposing of blasphemers and witches. The fire was typically kept small so the victim wouldn't die of asphyxiation too early in the process. The modern homophobic slur "faggot" is thought to derive from the Old French term for the small bundle of sticks used to make the fire: *fagot*.

To Justify Capital Punishment

And if any mischief follow, then thou shalt give life for life, Eye for eye, tooth for tooth, hand for hand, foot for foot, Burning for burning, wound for wound, stripe for stripe. (Exodus 21:23-25)

Ye have heard that it hath been said, An eye for an eye, and a tooth for a tooth: But I say unto you, That ye resist not evil; but whosoever shall smite thee on thy right cheek, turn to him the other also. (Matthew 5:38-39)

Once more we observe in these polar opposite passages our old nemesis, the conflict between Old and New Testament principles. But just as before, it presents no problem for Christians because, as we have seen time and again, they are experts at selective application of Jesus's teachings.

But wait! The conflict runs deeper. The Fifth Commandment states clearly, "Thou shalt not kill." Again, no worries. Christians learned long ago to read this as "thou shalt not *murder*," and to view the execution of capital criminals as a dispassionate ministerial act in which they are God's agent of justice. And though they briefly lost the support of the U.S. Supreme Court on this point during the 1970s, they quickly managed to regain it, along with the approval of a majority of all Americans.

To Assign Guilt for Disease Outbreaks

> And Azariah the chief priest, and all the priests, looked upon him, and, behold, he was leprous in his forehead, and they thrust him out from thence; yea, himself hasted also to go out, because the Lord had smitten him. And Uzziah the king was a leper unto the day of his death, and dwelt in a several house, being a leper; for he was cut off from the house of the Lord... (II Chronicles 26:20-21)

You will have to excuse a certain degree of overlap with other entries here and elsewhere, because this business of attributing natural phenomena to God's wrath comes up a lot. Why? It's simple really: because correlation *is* causation. This same principle underlies the scientific discovery that washing your car is the cause of all rain.

So let's get started with every last one of you admitting the obvious. If your father died of heart disease, it was because he was evil. If your mother died of Alzheimer's disease, it was because she was evil. If your spouse died of cancer, it was because he or she was evil. And if your children have asthma, autism, or leukemia, let's face it, it's because they are evil. If you have diabetes, then you're evil too.

What's that you say? You're a regular church-goer? Well then! I take it all back. Why? Because *there are rules.* And one of those rules is that disease could never be God's punishment for being a good Christian. This is why no one ever said the Black Death was God's punishment for driving the Muslims from Western Europe, and no one ever claimed malaria was God's way of punishing missionaries for Christianizing indigenous peoples.

No, those were just flukes. In contrast, here are just a few of the disease outbreaks from history that Christians claimed were God's punishment for the sins of the afflicted:

- *The plague of Justinian* (sixth century): as described above, the Christian emperor Justinian the Great attributed this pandemic to widespread homosexuality.

- *The bubonic plague* (fourteenth to sixteenth centuries): some blamed it on the prevalence of witchcraft in Europe, others on the ubiquitous Jews who refused to convert to Christianity.

- *The English cholera epidemic of 1832:* coincided with the early days of the temperance movement and was said to be an expression of God's displeasure with excessive alcohol consumption.

- *The Spanish flu pandemic of 1918:* Christian clergy claimed it was God's punishment for a changing, post-Victorian culture that saw the rise of Hollywood, the introduction of jazz music, and the arrival of various abstract art movements, among other racy social developments.

In modern times virtually every disease scare that has arisen, from SARS to Ebola to H1N1, has been the subject of endless TV evangelist and Christian spokesperson speculation on the role played by sin in the epidemic, aided by references to the many Bible stories that reinforce the linkage.

> And it was so, that...the hand of the Lord was against the city with a very great destruction: and he smote the men of the city, both small and great, and they had emerods [tumors] in their secret parts. (1 Samuel 5:9)

But of course nothing in ancient or modern times could compare to the self-righteous pontification inspired by STD outbreaks originating in mankind's "secret parts," and no STD will ever top HIV/AIDS for inspiring the rabid condemnation of the religious right. Those who have claimed a causal relationship between God's disapproval of LGBT lifestyles and HIV/AIDS include Pat Robertson, Jerry Falwell, head of the Southern Baptist Convention Charles Stanley, and even the beloved Billy Graham (who later apologized).

What is strange about this is that no other proven behavioral link to disease ever seems to take on quite these same biblical dimensions—only sexual activity. For example, you cannot work the correlation backward to determine that poor diet or lack of exercise are sinful, even though they are both closely linked to heart disease. Folks, once again the explanation is simple: *there are rules!* And another one of those rules is that you simply can't do that.

Now if you'll excuse me, I'm starting to feel sick.

To Assign Guilt for Natural Disasters

It's no surprise that Christians often explain natural disasters in identical fashion, cruelly sifting through the rubble for a group of sinners to blame the same way a bridge player searches a large hand of playing cards for trump. We see it in news media with every new calamity. Recent examples include the following tragedies:

- The 2013 typhoon in the Philippines, which was God's punishment for tolerance of prostitution and homosexuality according to the so-called True Christian Blog.

- The 2011 tsunami in Japan, which inspired TV news personality Glenn Beck to remark "What God does is God's business. But I'll tell you this—there's a message being sent. And that is, 'Hey, you know that stuff we're doing? Not really working out real well. Maybe we should stop doing some of it.' I'm just saying."

- The 2010 earthquake in Haiti that killed well over 100,000 people, which televangelist Pat Robertson said was God's punishment for when Haitians "got together and swore a pact to the devil. They said, 'We will serve you if you free us from the French.' True story. And so the devil said 'OK, it's a deal.'"

- The 2007 floods in the United Kingdom, which the Right Reverend Graham Dow claimed were God's punishment for tolerance of homosexuality.

- Hurricane Katrina in 2005, which caused Pastor John Hagee, the leader of the Christian Zionist movement in the United States, to remark "All hurricanes are acts of God, because God controls the heavens. I believe that New Orleans had a level of sin that was offensive to God, and they were recipients of the judgment of God for that." Topping the list of sins cited by church leaders was the city's sponsorship of the gay pride event known as Southern Decadence.

- The 2004 Indian Ocean tsunami in which nearly a quarter million people of every race from all over the world and every walk of life and faith were killed in fourteen different countries. This one is kind of obvious, don't you think? OK, I'll spell it out for you. According to its website GodHatesFags.com, the Westboro

Baptist Church claimed it "was an adumbration of the wrath of God, a harbinger of things to come."

And that's just in the past ten years. Of course no one from the Christian community said a word when a giant statue of Jesus along highway I-75 in Ohio between Cincinnati and Dayton was struck by lightning and caught on fire in 2010 (you can watch it burn on YouTube). And no one suggested God played a role in the devastating 2013 forest fires near Colorado Springs, Colorado, a haven for Evangelical Christian organizations. Don't forget those rules we mentioned in the prior section!

The first Christian revenge disaster was the story of Noah and the flood. I'm not going to itemize the hundreds of scientific and engineering reasons why the story simply must be understood as a metaphor, although I could. Neither will I list the dozens of other cultures which feature highly similar flood myths, although it would be easy to do. I will simply point out that many Jewish scholars believe the story of Noah was less a warning about the vengefulness of God than it was a counter-narrative to the Sumerian flood myth from the Epic of Gilgamesh, which preceded it. That story spoke of man's powerlessness in the face of capricious gods. Noah's story, on the other hand, was supposedly meant as a reminder of the importance of human agency in determining the ultimate fate of the world. That's something we all might want to contemplate as we slow-cook our planet.

To Oppose Life-Saving Medical Treatment

As I mentioned in part three of this book, two denominations have dominated this category of Christian madness for the past century: the Christian Scientists and the Jehovah's Witnesses. And though an exasperated society might gladly absorb the death of a few adult followers out of respect for their First Amendment right to believe whatever foolish thing they choose, the court battles in this area lamentably tend to focus on their right as parents to refuse medical treatment to their innocent children.

Thankfully the law has evolved to the point where in most states government health officials are permitted to seek court approval for compelling the treatment of children. In some cases criminal complaints, including murder charges, have been filed against parents who did not comply. Unfortunately, gray areas remain. For example, there is a 2013 Ohio case involving an Amish girl named Sarah, whose parents removed her from a cancer facility, claiming the treatments were "killing" their daughter. Their lawyers claimed the law ought to provide them sufficient parental and religious prerogative to make such a choice.

If you have ever watched a loved one go through the agony of chemotherapy and radiation treatments, you can understand the poignancy of this dilemma. The Amish family has gone into hiding, and their case is ongoing. If you're inclined toward prayer, pray for this little girl. Believe me, no child should have to go through that dreadful ordeal.

To Oppose Science

Science and the Christian Church have a long history of antagonism dating back at least to the rise of Copernicus's theory of heliocentrism—the idea that the sun, not the earth, is at the center of the solar system—in the sixteenth century. (See "The Trial of Galileo Galilei" in part five, below.) But nothing really compares to the firestorm of Christian controversy the publication of Charles Darwin's seminal book, *On the Origin of the Species*, ignited when it was published in 1859.

As should be painfully obvious to anyone with a television or a computer connected to the Internet, many Christians have a serious problem with Darwin's theory of natural selection, also commonly known as evolution. The reason is it conflicts with the creation story (or stories) found in the Old Testament book of Genesis. Christian opposition to evolution theory is so extreme that some of them concocted a pseudo-science known as intelligent design theory to refute it. While I do not wish to belabor this very tiresome subject, I do feel it is necessary to make two important points about the anti-science stance of so many churches.

First, the Fundamentalist obsession with referring to evolution as "just a theory, not a fact" misses an important point: in the jargon of scientists, evolution is both a theory *and* a fact. A theory is a proposed explanation for a given phenomenon whose predictions are repeatedly tested by peer-reviewed experimentation, for example the theory* that objects fall due to gravity. A fact is an observation that, after being subjected to rigorous empirical analysis, has gained widespread acceptance in the scientific community, for example the fact that objects fall due to gravity. If Fundamentalist simpletons cannot grasp these basics, how could they ever hope to fathom the *fact* that proofs exist for both wave and particle *theories* of light? The truth is that much of what science knows, it knows somewhat tenuously. But that does not stop it from working wonders, and narrow gaps in scientific certainty do not endow stupid, superstitious people with the inalienable right to pick and choose what is factual.

The second point is this: on August 21, 2013, an employee of the Creation Museum in Petersburg, Kentucky was struck by lightning on museum grounds. God has spoken. Who are we to ask questions?

*According to the science page of the August 17, 2005 issue of the farcical newspaper *The Onion*, this theory is under fire from evangelical scientists claiming that objects drop to the ground due to "intelligent falling."

To Justify War

The Lord is a man of war: the Lord is his name. (Exodus 15:3)

Blessed are the peacemakers: for they shall be called the children of God. (Matthew 5:9)

Onward, Christian soldiers…marching as to war…with the cross of Jesus…going on before! (1864 hymn by Sabine Baring-Gould)

What have we here? Why, it's that monkey wrench in the machinery, the grinding clash between the bloody fist of Yahweh and the gentle touch of Jesus, and we know who normally wins that particular war.

Don't get me wrong. It's not like Christianity invented this business of waging war in the name of God. According to historian Jared Diamond, the existence of official state religions has always facilitated war. How? By making troops "willing to fight suicidally." He observes that "what makes patriotic and religious fanatics such dangerous opponents is not the deaths of the fanatics themselves, but their willingness to accept the deaths of a fraction of their number in order to annihilate or crush their infidel enemy." J. Diamond, *Guns, Germs, and Steel: The Fates of Human Societies*, (New York: Norton, 1999), p. 270. War in the name of God works so well it might be easier to list the major wars of history *not* fought on religious grounds, but that's no excuse for flouting Christianity's bedrock tenets.

Here is Christianity's supposed excuse, delivered by Saint Augustine way back in the fifth century. In his writings he developed the concept of a "just war" that should be waged by a proper, recognized authority against a recognized evil and said that under such circumstances, Christians could go to war on God's behalf, with peace as the objective. But while the idea of a just war makes perfect secular sense in a civil society, it makes no Christian sense at all in light of the plain message of Jesus's famed Sermon on the Mount.

Every good Christian knows those rules. "You have heard that it was said, 'An eye for an eye and a tooth for a tooth.' But I say to you, Do not resist one who is evil" (Matthew 5:38-39). "You have heard that it was said, 'You shall love your neighbor and hate your enemy.' But I say to you, Love your enemies and pray for those who persecute you" (Matthew 5: 43-44). That's crystal clear. However, as we have seen time and again, *they* get to pick when a departure from Jesus's message is warranted, and *we* are not allowed to question it.

How does one tell when a war is just? It's simple, really. Just ask yourself if we are the ones fighting it. This was true right from the beginning, when America fought its first bloody war, over—ahem—unjust taxation: "It is the object only of war that makes it honorable. And if there was ever a just war since the world began, it is this in which America is now engaged" (Thomas Paine, "The American Crisis," March 21, 1778).

With our society's moral guardians standing ever ready to support rather than oppose war, we appear doomed to everlasting repetition of the cycle captured in this Old Testament verse from the book of Ecclesiastes, popularized in the 1965 hit single by The Byrds:

> A time to love, and a time to hate;
> a time of war, and a time of peace.

So there's a time to follow Jesus and a time to turn away, "Turn, Turn, Turn" over and over again. Maybe this is what is meant by the term Judeo-Christian ethic. It is a toggle switch—Judeo in times of war, Christian in times of peace. A time of peace? I swear it's already too late for the estimated quarter billion war dead throughout history, vast numbers of them due to Christian-on-Christian wars no less. Far too many of them died needlessly. History has shown that war may at times be necessary, but it should never be considered holy.

To Justify Theft of Lands

History has witnessed many great land grabs in the name of this or that god, but few were bigger or bolder than America's expansionist march from the Mississippi River to the Pacific Ocean. We even gave it a name: Manifest Destiny.

Journalist John L. Sullivan popularized the concept, which grew out of the Second Great Awakening period of American hyper-religiosity.

In an 1839 column predicting a great expansion of the influence of American ideals, Sullivan coined the term "divine destiny." He later switched it to "manifest destiny" in an 1845 article urging the US annexation of Texas based on divine providence, i.e. a gift from God.

The New World Encyclopedia entry on Manifest Destiny states that it:

> ...comprised not only a mandate for territorial expansionism, but also notions of individualism, idealism, American Exceptionalism, Romantic nationalism, White supremacism, and a belief in the inherent greatness of what was then called the Anglo-Saxon race.

Its key themes were:

> 1) the virtue of the American people and their institutions,

> 2) the mission to spread these institutions, thereby redeeming and remaking the world in the image of the U.S., and

> 3) the destiny under God to accomplish this work.

(Eye roll...sigh)

While Manifest Destiny never achieved the status of formal US policy, it was an influential political force throughout the territorial expansionist era leading up to the Civil War, when US borders finally reached from sea to shining sea. The lasting problem is this: it left behind the aforementioned cross-eyed bastard child, American exceptionalism, the pervasive notion that God has graced this country with some kind of *carte blanche* for its actions. This is beyond regrettable given that God stood quietly by while we as a country committed many grave mistakes in the past—the Native American genocide, slavery, Jim Crow, abuse of the environment, maltreatment of women and children...need I continue?—and that the only thing stopping us from making even more errors is our ongoing capacity for sound reasoning and good conscience, not God's will for heaven's sake.

To Justify Extreme Accumulations of Wealth

> Keep your life free from love of money, and be content with what you have." (Hebrews 13:5)

Bible verses like this seem plain enough (see also the verses below in part six), but Christians have a long history of building large fortunes in the name of the Lord. What started out as perhaps the world's first religion to worship a deity born into poverty, one which actively encouraged its followers to sell their possessions and freely give their money to the poor, somehow warped into a faith in which the accumulation of wealth was not only accepted, it was openly encouraged.

There have been many dogmatic shifts in Christian history. Some of them were quite dramatic, such as the abandonment of strict adherence to Jewish orthodoxy, as described earlier. But given Jesus's repeated, unmistakable warnings about the evils of greed, materialism, and money, topping this 180-degree reversal would require something along the lines of a Satan-worshippers-for-Christ movement. It is truly shocking and shameful.

Among the first to crack open the door to benign accumulation of wealth was the beloved and influential thirteenth century Italian theologian Thomas Aquinas. Unlike his predecessor Saint Jerome, who at times suggested that great wealth was literally the equivalent of theft, Aquinas rejected the absolute condemnation of riches, writing that what was unacceptable before God was not wealth per se, but the immoderate desire for wealth. OK, that's not what Jesus said, but continue please.

Elaborating, Aquinas stated that it is acceptable for a Christian "to have external riches, in so far as they are necessary for him to live *in keeping with his condition of life*" (emphasis added). He went on to say:

> It is thus appropriate for an aristocrat to seek to have more money than a peasant, etc. What continues to be unacceptable, however, is desire for more than what is appropriate to one's station, or indeed *the desire to change station, to improve one's social condition.* (Emphasis added) (Aquinas, S.T., II, II, q. 117, quoted in A. Kahan, *Mind vs. Money*, (New Brunswick: Transaction Publishers, 2010), p. 48)

Is it really necessary to state how messed up this is? In any case, the horse was out of the barn, and next came centuries of the pursuit, aggregation, and hoarding of wealth by Christians, never mind the teachings of Jesus. Vows of poverty were thought to be for monastic orders like the Franciscans and Dominicans.

Which brings us to today, when televangelist and best-selling author Joel Osteen can make statements like this without fear of Christian backlash: "God wants us to prosper financially, to have plenty of money, to fulfill the destiny he has laid out for us." Perhaps Osteen, whose personal fortune is estimated at $40 million, neglected to mention that the "us" in his statement was a reference to his own family and inner circle.

He is not alone, however. There is a theological movement known as the Prosperity Gospel, or Health and Wealth Gospel, which holds that financial blessing is the reward for performance of a Christian's contract with God, in which faithfulness and righteous living (including, of course, generous donations to one's church) are the quid pro quo. Influential leaders of the movement have included the scandal-plagued Robert Tilton, the late Oral Roberts, and the aptly named Creflo Dollar (yes, I'm serious).

The absurdity of basing a Christian school of thought on a literal contradiction of Jesus's teachings is almost beneath commentary, but a

2014 opinion piece by Cathleen Falsani in the *Washington Post* held its nose long enough to declare the Prosperity Gospel one of "the worst ideas of the decade."

The decade? Try the last two millennia.

To Exploit the Environment

> And God said to unto them, Be fruitful, and multiply, and replenish the earth, and subdue it: and have dominion over the fish of the sea, and over the fowl of the air, and over every living thing.... (Genesis 1:28)

With Bible passages like this encouraging them, Christians have spent two thousand years doing exactly that: subduing the Earth. Now there is hardly a corner that remains unexploited. Granted, they had lots of help from the rest of the human race, but it was Christians, in their own inimitable style, who had the audacity to disguise their insatiable lust for land and natural resources as the literal fulfillment of God's will.

Need convincing? Then I give you the case of James Watt, who served as Ronald Reagan's secretary of the interior from January 1981 to November 1983. His job was to oversee the Bureau of Land Management, which controls tens of millions of acres of federal lands, and the National Park Service. While in office, he set an agency record (not broken until the second Bush administration) for fewest species granted federal protection during his tenure. Greg Whetstone, the chief environmental counsel to the House Energy and Commerce Committee at the time, referred to him as one of the most "blatantly anti-environmental political appointees" in American history.

Watt's other signature achievements during his term included quintupling the federal land areas leased to coal mining companies, resisting private donations of land to the federal government for conservational purposes, restructuring his Department of the Interior to reduce its regulatory power, dramatically increasing the leasing of offshore drilling rights, and decreasing funding for federal environmental protection programs. In 2008 *Time* magazine named him the sixth worst cabinet member in the entire history of the United States.

And this is how he testified before Congress in 1981:

> That is the delicate balance the Secretary of the Interior must have: to be steward for the natural resources for this generation as well as future generations. *I do not know how many future generations we can count on before the Lord returns*; whatever it is we have to manage with a skill to leave the resources needed for future generations. (Emphasis added) (Testimony before the House Interior Committee on February 5, 1981)

So whether it was two generations, three generations, or—God only knows—ten or even fifteen, James Watt was going to make sure we didn't use it *all* up before Jesus returned in glory.

Think that's a joke? Here's another one, even funnier: "My responsibility is to follow the Scriptures, which call upon us to occupy the land until Jesus returns." (Watt quoted in *The Washington Post*, May 24, 1981.)

How does one even react to something so frivolous, so sanctimonious, so utterly galling? Perhaps with the same mixture of resentment and resignation Native American Chief Seattle conveyed in his treaty oration to the Governor of Washington Territory (a Department of the Interior employee) in 1854:

> The white man's God cannot love our people or he would protect them. They seem to be orphans who can look nowhere for help. How then can we be brothers? How can your God become our God and renew our prosperity and awaken us in dreams of returning greatness? If we have a common Heavenly Father He must be partial, for He came to His paleface children. We never saw him. He

gave you laws but he had no word for His red children whose teeming multitudes once filled this vast continent as stars fill the firmament...Your religion was written upon tablets of stone by the iron finger of your God so that you could not forget. The Red Man could never comprehend or remember it. (Reproduced in the *Seattle Sunday Star* on October 29, 1887.)

Don't feel bad, Chief Seattle. There are times when the rest of us struggle with it, too.

***

It's a charming résumé, is it not? Feel free to add your own. Historical examples, that is, not fresh abuses. The world has had enough of the latter. And while it bears repeating that some of these atrocities are not exclusive to Christianity, it nonetheless remains a sordid and shameful legacy for which every Christian is continually bound to apologize and compensate. In this sense, the extreme humility advocated by biblical figures like Jesus and John the Baptist ought to serve modern Christians very well indeed.

If you are known by the company you keep, what do these horrible, hateful friends of Christianity tell us about the faith? So explain to me again how wonderful your world is, you infernal Fundamentalist.

PART FIVE

KNOW THE CHURCH SCANDALS

Now let's look at some of the more sensational examples of egregious Vatican misconduct, ignorance, and neglect. I almost feel bad singling out the Roman Catholic Church for this kind of rough treatment, but considering that the story essentially starts with them, and that Catholicism drove the bus, so to speak, for over a thousand years, and given that it does tend to be the most pompous of the various Christian brands, I will give it the VIP treatment it is accustomed to. Here is an unlucky baker's dozen of some—but not nearly all—of the worst moments in the Vatican's long and sordid history.

The following examples should serve you well in any argument about morality with a devout Catholic. And remember, these aren't just sometimes hilarious, sometimes sickening, always fascinating historical anecdotes. They feature figures many of whom are for some reason *still* revered by the Church. Their graves are not pissed on, their portraits are not slashed, and statues of them are not toppled and broken to pieces. On the contrary, some are still honored with ceremony, and their papal orders in some cases continue to bind the Church. Here we go, hang on to your butt.

The Cadaver Synod

In 897 A.D. Pope Steven VI conducted this bizarre trial featuring accusations of heresy against his predecessor, Pope Formosus. Why bizarre? Because it was held nine months *after* Formosus's death! Steven had the deceased pontiff's decomposing corpse exhumed, dressed it in papal garments, and actually seated it in court as a defendant. After pronouncing a guilty verdict, he ordered the three fingers Formosus used for issuing papal blessings cut off of his dead hand. The cadaver was eventually tossed into the Tiber River, then later fished out and re-buried by his remaining loyalists.

Goodbye Antipope, Hello Pope

Not long after the Cadaver Synod, Pope Sergius III (who served from 904 to 911 A.D.) came to power after having his predecessor, whom he had proclaimed an "antipope," strangled to death. His own cardinals called him "the slave of every vice." His son by a teenaged mistress, a prostitute named Marozia who was thirty years his junior, succeeded him as Pope John XI.

The Boy Pope

Continuing a nightmarish "dark century" for the office, Pope John XII (who served from 955 to 964 A.D.) was a mere eighteen-year-old when he assumed the papacy. One church historian described him as "the very dregs" of those who have served. According to the "Patrologia Latina," a huge collection of ecclesiastical commentaries spanning roughly one thousand years, the charges levied against John included invoking demons to punish his enemies, compulsive gambling, and turning the papal living quarters into the equivalent of a whorehouse. He was also rumored to be an arsonist and a literal murderer. Author and Vatican observer E.R. Chamberlain referred to him as "a Christian Caligula whose crimes were rendered particularly horrific by the office he held." His acts of adultery allegedly included sex with several of his family members. John reportedly died in bed with a married woman, some say of a stroke, others say at the hands of her angry husband.

Ahead of His Time

Pope Benedict IX (who served from 1032 to 1048) took power when he was only twenty years old, having essentially inherited the title by virtue of being the nephew of two previous popes, John XIX and Benedict VIII. At the end of his reign, he became the only pontiff ever to sell off his papacy—the buyer was Pope Gregory VI.

Benedict shocked even the most hardened Vatican residents by repeatedly debauching young boys right in the Lateran Palace. After momentarily finding religion and abdicating the papacy to live in a monastery, he later changed his mind and seized power all over again with the help of his family's private army. He was, in the words of the eleventh century Catholic cardinal and reformer Saint Peter Damian, "a demon from hell in the disguise of a priest" who "feasted on immorality." Considering the Church is again embroiled in molestation scandals, it seems the more things change in Catholicism, the more they stay the same.

Would You Like Some Fresh-Ground Pepper With That?

Power-mad Pope Boniface VIII, in his papal bull of 1302 titled "Unam Sanctum," proclaimed that "it is absolutely necessary for salvation that every human creature be subject to the Roman pontiff"—a lunatic rant that may represent the outermost claim of papal supremacy in the long, egotistical history of the Church. When his critics, including the prominent and powerful Colonna family, bristled at this, he ordered the massacre of the entire population of the Colonnas' hometown of Palestrina. He did so after procuring the town's surrender with promises that it would be spared. After killing every inhabitant, he razed the vacant town to the ground and, for good measure, he *salted* it.

When not slaughtering his subjects, he was said to enjoy *ménages à trois* with a local married woman and her daughter. He supposedly once remarked that sex with boys or women was no worse than rubbing one hand against the other. His reign as pope, which lasted from 1294 to 1303, was immortalized in Dante's *Divine Comedy,* in which the author positioned Boniface in the eighth circle of hell.

Pope Sixtus IV: A Tale of Syphilis and Simony

This pope, who served as head of the Roman Church from 1471 to 1484, is fondly remembered for commissioning the Sistine Chapel and transforming the Vatican from a medieval wreck into a Renaissance jewel. Unfortunately, he was also responsible for initiating the Spanish Inquisition, for attempting to revive the Crusades against the Turks, and for taking nepotism and simony (the sale of lucrative church positions and sacraments) to unconscionable new levels. In 1478 he was allegedly involved in a conspiracy to murder several members of the powerful Medici family at High Mass in the Duomo in Florence before a huge crowd of worshippers. He was also rumored to be an advanced syphilitic, the father of numerous illegitimate children, including one with his older sister, and an active bisexual. The Italian historian and local judge Stefano Infessura referred to Sixtus in 1484 as a "lover of boys and sodomites." Perhaps he could serve as patron saint to the pedophiles of the modern Church.

History's First Blood Transfusion

The perversely-named Pope Innocent VIII, who served as pope from 1484 to 1492, acknowledged eight illegitimate sons, but was rumored to have many more. Among his signature achievements was a formal acknowledgement by papal bull of his belief in witchcraft and a call for more witch trials, as noted in part four of this book. On his deathbed he had the blood of three ten-year-old boys infused into his mouth. Paid a ducat apiece, all three died as a result. Despite frantic efforts by the Vatican to discredit the story, medical historians still cite it. Previous efforts to revive the dying pope had included employing a winsome young wet nurse to suckle him with her fresh breast milk.

The Worst of the Worst

It is truly difficult to pick just one, but most Church historians name Pope Alexander VI, a member of the notorious Borgia family, as the worst pope ever. Having procured his position by out-bribing his rivals, he served from 1492 to 1503.

Noted historian Edward Gibbon was fond of saying that Alexander presided over more orgies than masses. At the infamous 1501 Vatican orgy dubbed the Joust of the Whores, he and male family members reportedly tossed chestnuts on the floor for the women to root after like pigs, then awarded prizes of clothes and jewelry to whichever man could fornicate with the most of them. His hobbies included watching horses copulate, which reportedly caused him to erupt in fits of laughter. His papal accomplishments included naming his teenaged son a cardinal and validating Spain's absurd claim to ownership of the newly discovered Western Hemisphere. Another of his nine illegitimate children (Cesare) served as the model for Niccolo Machiavelli's notorious treatise on ruthless statecraft, *The Prince.*

Poisoning was suspected in his death, which may explain why his body decomposed with unusual speed. Historian and theologian Raphael Volterrano, an eyewitness to this, wrote:

> It was a revolting scene to look at that deformed, blackened corpse, prodigiously swelled, and exhaling an infectious smell; his lips and nose were covered with brown drivel, his mouth was opened very widely, and his tongue, inflated by poison, fell out upon his chin; therefore no fanatic or devotee dared to kiss his feet or hands, as custom would have required.

After a comparatively brief stay at St. Peter's Basilica, Alexander's body was moved to another location because he was considered too evil to remain buried there.

From Fine Art to Fornication: Pope Julius II

Remembered for his patronage of Michelangelo and Raphael, Julius, who was the nephew of the notorious Pope Sixtus IV, served as pontiff from 1503 to 1513. Perhaps no other pope did as much to beautify the Vatican. Unfortunately, his eye for beauty also led him to father at least one illegitimate child. It was said that there was nothing of the priest about him but the Cossack, and he did not always wear that. He was nicknamed *il terribile* and rumored to be bisexual, which is not hard to imagine given his close relationship with the artist Michelangelo, who was well known to be a homosexual.

He was also allegedly tormented by sexually transmitted disease. The Conciliabulum of Pisa, organized by disgruntled church leaders in 1511 against Julius, renounced him as a "sodomite covered with shameful [i.e., syphilitic] ulcers."

Cash-and-Carry Redemption

Under the reign of *Pope Leo X,* the practice of selling indulgences for the forgiveness of sins reached its peak, leading ultimately to Martin Luther's fateful hammering of his Ninety-Five Theses to the door of the church in Wittenberg, Germany. The attitude of the Church at that time was epitomized in this quote from German Johann Tetzel, a Dominican priest tasked with raising money to finish St. Peter's Basilica in Rome through the sale of indulgences:

> *So wie das Geld im Kasten klingt;*
> *die Seele aus dem Fegfeuer springt.*

Here is the English translation:

> As soon as the gold in the coffer rings;
> the rescued soul from purgatory springs.

These fiscal policies of Leo X, who was made a cleric at age seven and a cardinal at age thirteen (and for the record kept a pet elephant named Hanno* at Vatican expense), led directly to the Protestant Reformation and one of the bloodiest periods of political instability in European history. For good measure, he once spent one-seventh of the Church's cash reserves on a single lavish ceremony for his own benefit. Some historians (for example Francesco Guicciardini) also believe he engaged in various homosexual affairs while in office.

It has to be said that if the church's experience with homosexuals were strictly limited to the madmen that have held its highest office, one could almost understand its cruel anti-homosexual policies. Needless to say, it most certainly is not.

*Hanno died of complications from a gold-laced treatment for severe constipation. I really wish it weren't true.

The Trial of Galileo Galilei

Galileo's work on advancing the Copernican theory that Earth is one of numerous planets in a solar system orbiting the sun led to his trial in Rome on charges of heresy in 1633. At the time he was sixty-eight years old and suffering from illness, so he accepted the church's generous offer to "abjure, curse, and detest" his own findings in public to save his own skin.

He lived under house arrest until his death in 1642, which was not nearly long enough to see the Church lift its ban on his book in 1822.

The Vatican finally saw fit to accept Galileo's findings in the 1960s, and in 1992, only 359 years after threatening to torture and imprison him (and a mere twenty-one years before the election of Francis, the first Pope with a science degree), the Church, speaking through Pope John Paul II, formally apologized for its actions in "The Galileo Affair."

Pope Pius XII: "Hitler's Pope"

The reign of Pius began in 1939, the year Hitler—coming from a Catholic upbringing—invaded Poland, and continued throughout World War II, a period of deafening silence from the church on the issue of ongoing German war atrocities. Despite a recent spate of apologist literature trying gamely to rehabilitate Pius's reputation, the fact remains that the Church, which didn't officially stop blaming the Jews for the death of Jesus until 1965 and didn't formally acknowledge the nation of Israel until 1993, has a lot of explaining to do for its anti-Semitic history and total passivity during the Jewish Holocaust.

The Present-Day Molestation Scandal

The horrifying full dimensions of this scandal are a topic for a different book. Suffice it to say there is nothing else remotely like it in modern Christian history: the knowing, deliberate institutional shielding of monstrous, predatory pedophiles. Truly the institutional arrogance underlying it boggles the mind. Consider the following timeline relating to allegations in just one case involving a certain Father Lawrence C. Murphy, abridged from a March 25, 2010 article in *The New York Times* (whose archives are a rich source of information on the wider scandal):

1950: Father Murphy was ordained a priest in May then accepted a position at St. John's School for the Deaf in St. Francis, Wisconsin as a chaplain.

1955-1963: According to fellow chaplain David Walsh, former St. John's students began alleging Murphy had abused them. Murphy first denied then confirmed the allegations to the archbishop of Milwaukee. At this point a sane organization would have called the police.

January 1, 1963: But who said anything about sane? Murphy was *promoted* to the top job at the school and served as its director for the next eleven years, even though his superiors were already receiving complaints from students that he was molesting them.

1974: a group of former students passed out mock "WANTED" posters of Murphy outside a cathedral in Milwaukee with the aim of warning the public and pressuring the Church to stop him from working around children.

September 12, 1974: Murphy's superiors sent him to live at his family's Boulder Junction country home in Northern Wisconsin, calling it a "temporary sick leave" in an accompanying memo. He never returned to St. John's after twenty-four years there.

1974-1993: The extent of Murphy's contact with young boys is unclear, but according to *The New York Times*, Murphy "interacted freely with children" during this period. The *Times* quoted Donald Marshall of West Allis, Wisconsin, saying that after being sent to a juvenile detention center in 1977 or 1978 for offenses he committed as a minor, he was molested in his holding cell by Murphy, who was serving the institution as a chaplain. Marshall reported the incident immediately, but nothing was done. The *Times* quoted another victim anonymously who claimed to have been molested as a minor at Murphy's Boulder Junction lake cottage during this period. Murphy also assisted at St. Anne's in the Boulder Junction area and possibly other parishes until 1994, when the Archdiocese of Milwaukee finally ordered him to stop.

December 12, 1993: The church at long last had Murphy evaluated by an expert in sexual disorders. After four days of interviews, she reported that he admitted to abusing nineteen children but likely had as many as two hundred victims. She observed that he did not appreciate the harm he caused, was unrepentant, and would likely resist treatment. She therefore concluded that the Church should re-evaluate having Murphy ever work again in parishes.

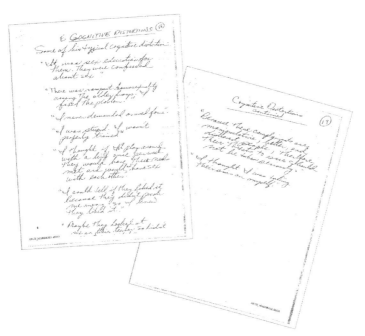

"There was rampant homosexuality among the older boys. I fixed the problem." "I thought I was taking their sins on myself."

July 17, 1996: Archbishop Weakland of Milwaukee wrote to Cardinal Joseph Ratzinger—yes *that* Cardinal Ratzinger, the future Pope Benedict XVI*—who at that time served as head of the Vatican office processing such complaints. Weakland notified him of the allegations of abuse against Murphy and suggested that the process of removing him from the priesthood be initiated. Nothing is done.

*After he became Pope, it was revealed that as a teenager Ratzinger, who is German, *had served in the Hitler Youth*, but this page can only bear so much ironic weight, so we will leave that subject to another day.

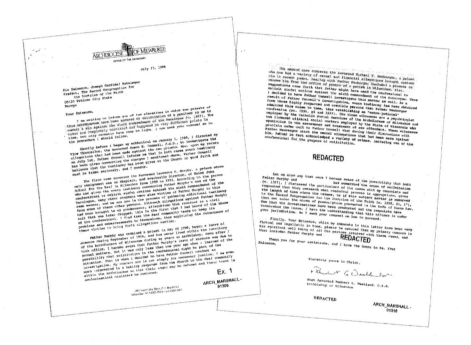

Letter showing Ratzinger as addressee.

March 10, 1997: Weakland wrote a second letter, this one to the Supreme Tribunal of the Apostolic Signatura in Rome, complaining that he'd received no response from Ratzinger, calling the matter "urgent," and saying that scandal and litigation were likely imminent. He asked for a waiver that would permit an accelerated trial against Murphy.

March 24, 1997: Archbishop Bertone, second in command to Ratzinger, finally authorized the trial but invoked church rules mandating secret proceedings.

January 12, 1998: Murphy wrote directly to Ratzinger, the future pope, pointing to a technicality in those same rules requiring such a trial to occur within one month of the offense, and boo-hooing that he was an old man in poor health. He asked that since the allegations were old and he had long ago repented he be allowed to live out his remaining years "in the dignity of my priesthood."

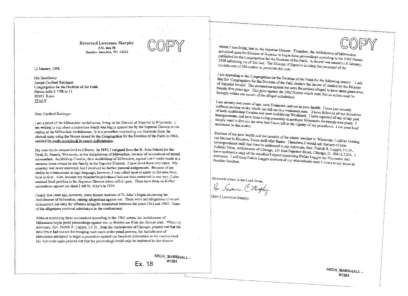

Again showing Ratzinger as addressee.

April 6, 1998: In response to Murphy's letter, Bertone, acting on Ratzinger's behalf, urged that the disciplinary proceedings be halted and replaced by "pastoral measures."

May 13, 1998: Bishop Fliss of the Superior, Wisconsin archdiocese responded to Bertone, saying that "all pastoral methods have been exhausted" in Murphy's case, and the "scandal cannot be sufficiently repaired, nor justice sufficiently restored, without a judicial trial against Fr. Murphy."

May 30, 1998: Weakland and Fliss met in Rome with Bertone and other Vatican officials, who gently instructed the two men to discontinue the proceedings against Murphy despite Weakland's protestations.

August 19, 1998: Murphy's formal trial was halted and replaced by an administrative proceeding to have him declared "irregular for ministry," whatever that is.

August 21, 1998: Murphy graciously died, sparing everyone further hand-wringing. His family defied an agreement to give him a closed-casket private funeral and instead held an open-casket public Mass with Murphy dressed in full vestments.

At no point did Church officials ever contact the police or the prosecutor's office.

And that is just one case. *One!* Out of how many? Here are some relevant figures from a March 13, 2013 story in *USA Today*:

- At least 6,905 Catholic clergy have been accused of sexual abuse since 1950. *6,905!*

- At least 16,463 victims of Catholic clergy sexual abuse have been identified. *16,463!*

- The Catholic Church has paid at least $2.5 billion in settlements, therapy bills, attorney fees, and other costs. Terrible.

And what is so terrible about the astronomical sum the Church has paid to date? Let me tell you: *it is way, way too small, that's what.* According to an August 3, 2013 article in the *National Post of Canada*, during the 1990's the Roman Catholic Church had, just for starters, at least four times that much—$10 billion—invested in foreign banking, insurance, steel, construction, and real estate companies, and it is reasonable to think that figure has at least doubled since. In addition, check this out, it owns 276,561 *square miles* of real estate—an area larger that the state of Texas. At a paltry $1,000 per acre, that would be worth $177 billion. And we haven't even gotten to the gold, silver, jewels, and warehouse-loads of priceless artwork and historical artifacts on which it is sitting.

No, the church hasn't paid enough. Not anywhere near enough. Imagine for a moment it was *your* sweet, beautiful, innocent son, the one *you* gave birth to or watched being born, *your* little angel, your angel *struggling with a handicap* no less, in the clutches of these monsters. Go ahead, stop reading and imagine it. *Think hard.* We'll wait right here for you…

Waiting…waiting…waiting…waiting…

Oh, the shock, the uncontrollable rage, the tumult! Oh, the irreparable damage and the endless repercussions! Oh, the fiendish depravity and the everlasting shame of it all! This! This…thing! THIS is engraved in your sweet child's mind, in his memory, in his personal history, in his personality. Not just in his, also in yours. And it is never coming out. Never! Oh, the shame! Oh, the shame, shame, shame, shame, shame!

***

And there you have it. You have now stockpiled more nuclear force than a Cold War superpower for terminating a Catholic moral scold with extreme prejudice. You might even find a way to work some of this into a debate over who should win the Notre Dame-USC football game. But let's never forget that this ammunition came at a terrible cost: the lost innocence and bodily integrity of those poor little boys who were molested. May those victims, many of whom are still alive, someday salvage a workable inner peace. And while we're at it, may the Church someday rediscover its own principles, stop blaming victims and making lame excuses, and finally throw itself pitifully on the ground in ashes and sackcloth and beg the world for forgiveness and mercy.

Don't hold your breath.

PART SIX

KNOW THE VERSES ON CHRISTIAN VIRTUE

Let's say you are trying to attend a sporting event, a concert, or just your garden variety zombie parade for Halloween, and suddenly there they are: the *Christian* zombies out for *your* brain, bearing megaphones, trying to ruin the party and scare your children with their glowering faces, grating voices, and damning rhetoric. What do you do? If you're like me, you don't suffer fools gladly, but engaging them in debate is usually a time-consuming mistake, and the show starts in ten minutes. You don't have time for a doctrinal cage match. You need to act fast and make it last; you need drive-by justice. And it is within your grasp, people. Just remember that it didn't happen for the Karate Kid overnight. Like any other system of self-defense, this one requires some training.

Folks, no one ever said it was easy to float like a butterfly and sting like a bee. To be properly prepared, you'll need to put in some work and memorize what I call the Verses on Christian Virtue—devastating passages from these chuckleheads' own Bible. Then, when you encounter Fundamentalist friendly fire, you can fight back with the verbal ninja star fit for the occasion. With these biblical bon mots you can inflict severe psychological pain from a safe distance while appearing as cool as Bruce Lee. (If you're feeling lazy, just carry my book around in your back pocket. This section has a colored edge for easy reference.)

Let's get to it. In each entry below, the biblical citation is listed right after because—pay attention here—you need to use it. It is chapter and verse citation to the Bible that really gets the attention of these freaks and endows you with authority in the eyes of neutral bystanders. Most of the verses are from Matthew, so it's usually just a matter of remembering a couple of numbers.

We'll begin with an all-time favorite. Here you have sarcastic Jesus at his very best, ripping sanctimonious religious leaders a new one without even breaking a sweat. I give you what is perhaps the most venomous take-down of self-righteous hypocrisy in in the entire Bible. Ready...aim...FIRE!

How can you say to your brother, "Let me take the speck out of your eye," when there is a log in your own eye? You hypocrite! First take the log out of your own eye, then you will see clearly to take the speck out of your brother's eye. (Matthew 7:5)

Glory hallelujah! This is a flashy quote, its authenticity is instantly recognizable, even to casual Christians, and it is right on the money.

You might want to repeat the good part to help it sink in—*You hypocrite! First take the log out of your own eye!* Ahhh...that felt good, didn't it?

But make no mistake, a hyped-up Christian clown soldier will come ready with at least one response—albeit garbled and incoherent—so you're still going to need back-up. Well here it is, my friend: a trusty left hook to go with that right cross, which serves as your farewell while you hurry to your seats just in time for tip-off.

Judge not lest ye be judged...you ignorant @$#%^&?!!!
[Insert expletive here at your discretion.] **(Matthew 7:1)**

This clincher is devastating in its simplicity, and it is widely known as both genuinely biblical (that first part of it anyway) and manifestly true. It strikes at the heart of everything these fools are doing and leaves them hung on the horns of the dilemma confronting all in-your-face Fundamentalists: how can they spitefully shame others in public without violating this direct order from Jesus?

And there you have it: a stinging two-part rebuke that restores some sanity to your world. Let freedom ring! Not freedom *of* speech mind you, freedom *from* speech—asinine speech. If you're ready for more, you might try taking wire cutters to their speaker cables. Or you might consider the following alternative pairing, likewise tailor made for holier-than-thou Christian displays.

Beware of practicing your piety before men in order to be seen by them; for then you will have no reward from your father who is in heaven. (Matthew 6:1)

It's starting to register with them now. You brought a gun to their knife fight. And what's worse, you're using *their ammunition*. But by now you know that these stiffs don't go down easy, so here is the *coup de grâce*:

When you pray, do not be like the hypocrites, for they love to pray standing in synagogues and on street corners to be seen by others. (Matthew 6:5)

(In Matthew this passage continues in the same rich vein, adding "When you pray, go into your room, close the door and pray to your Father." Oh Jesus, you were a genius!)

It is the "street corner" reference that drops them dead, since that is quite literally where they are standing. It's beautiful, I tell you, beautiful. Be creative, do a touchdown dance, bust a rhyme!

And when y'all pray, don' be like no hypocrite,
Cuz they standin' on the corner like hos and shit.

Yes, knowing just this pair of combinations ought to make you the Mike Tyson of street confrontations, and be more than enough for ninety-nine percent of the public situations that arise. But for the advanced combatant, I'll offer a few other deadly weapons to keep in your arsenal.

***

For those excruciating moments when someone has control of a microphone in public and exploits the situation with an interminable prayer or blessing:

And in praying do not heap up empty phrases like the Gentiles do; for they think that they will be heard for their many words. (Matthew 6:7)

Warning: sarcastic use of this verse will probably get you thrown out of most wedding receptions, could result in loss of leftover food privileges at holiday meals, and might start a riot if used during the invocation at a NASCAR race, where local preachers have been known to give long-winded thanks for everything from American servicemen to the sport's sanctioning body to the generous sponsorship of the local grocery chain, all in the name of Jesus. Or, to paraphrase Ricky Bobby's prayer from *Talladega Nights*, "In the name of eight pound, six ounce, newborn *baby* Jesus…Powerade is delicious… Amen!"

***

Whenever Christian hatemongers advocate violence or revenge against anybody, or austere policies towards the poor, the unlucky, the undocumented, or even criminals seeking mercy, they really deserve an earful of the following:

If any one strikes you on the right cheek, turn to him the other also. (Matthew 5:39)

Just keep it coming:

And if anyone should sue you and take your coat, let him have your cloak as well. (Matthew 5:40)

And coming:

And if any one forces you to go one mile, go with him two miles. (Matthew 5:41)

For as long as it takes, because Christians deserve to be held to account for these, their own core principles. If they are sincere in their belief, this is where the rubber meets the road.

Give to him who begs from you, and do not refuse him who would borrow from you. (Matthew 5:42)

If you are lucky, your antagonist will respond by saying "Hey, the Lord helps those who help themselves." Ask him to show you where this line appears in his Bible (*hint: it doesn't*), then quietly back away from his frantic efforts to find it and disappear before he looks back up.

***

When a hard-core Christian tells you how great his or her church is, or for that matter, how great his or her family, friends, neighborhood, school, business, city, state, or country is, you should ask how that fits together with the following:

The last will be first, and the first last. (Matthew 20:16)

Here's some reinforcement in case your first attempt bounces off their beaming pride:

Blessed are the meek, for they shall inherit the Earth. (Matthew 5:5)

***

And for dealing with those who can't choose between worshipping the all-powerful Jesus and worshipping the almighty dollar—Joel Osteen take note—we present to you...drum roll please...*the Money Mantras!*

> Do not lay up for yourselves treasures on Earth, where moth and rust consume and where thieves break in and steal, but lay up for yourselves treasures in heaven. (Matthew 6:19-20)

Feeling greedy? Here's another:

> No one can serve two masters; for either he will hate the one and love the other, or he will be devoted to one and despise the other. You cannot serve God and mammon [money]. (Matthew 6:24)

And another:

> It is easier for a camel to go through the eye of a needle than for a rich man to enter the kingdom of God. (Matthew 19:24)

And another:

> When you give a feast, invite the poor, the maimed, the lame, the blind, and you will be blessed, because they cannot repay you. (Luke 14:13)

One more:

> [Jesus] said to him, "One thing you still lack. Sell all that you have and distribute to the poor, and you will have treasure in heaven; and come, follow me." But when he heard this he became sad, for he was very rich. (Luke 18:22-23)

And BOOM goes the dynamite. He's calling your name, Joel! There are plenty of other passages in which Jesus bad-mouths materialism. After all, it's one of his favorite themes. But these are the most quotable. And should gilded Christians balk at the invitation to divest themselves of their wealth, consider whipping out these redistribution retorts from the book of Acts.

And all who believed were together and had all things in common; and they sold their possessions and goods and distributed them to all, as any had need. (Acts 2:44)

Need some frosting on top? Try this:

There was not a needy person among them [earliest Christians], for as many as were possessors of lands or houses sold them, and brought the proceeds of what was sold and laid it at the apostles' feet; and distribution was made to each as any had need. (Acts 4:34-35)

Tough luck, Joel! It looks like your $10 million mansion in Houston really needs to go.

Anyone with lingering doubts about the seriousness of the early Christian call to communal living need only be reminded of the story of Anani'as (not the one from Damascus in Paul's story, see Acts 5:1-6), who sold his land to follow Jesus, but brought the Apostles only part of the proceeds, stashing the rest for himself...whereupon he promptly fell dead on the spot.

***

When you find yourself among a crowd of Christians who prefer a heavy dose of guns mixed in with their god, remind them of the following passages, plain as a bumper sticker on a pickup truck:

> **You have heard it said "An eye for an eye and a tooth for a tooth." But I say to you, do not resist one who is evil. (Matthew 5:38-39)**

Did they survive your first salvo? Fire another round, with this old standby:

> **He who lives by the sword shall perish by the sword. (Matthew 25:52)**

***

Now they've started to get personal, calling you wicked and accusing you of being a fornicator and a drunkard. OK, so they got off a few lucky shots. But that doesn't mean you have to take it lying down. If you're one of those people who like to use every club in the bag, here is a lesser-known verse good for those times when you get a megaphone-load of Old Testament invective, condemning what some Christian miscreant claims is your immorality.

A man is justified not by works of the law but through faith in Jesus Christ...because by works of the law no one will be justified. (Galatians 2:16)

In other words, these fools are preaching behavior when they should be preaching belief, and need to get their heads out of their butts and understand their own religion.

And for when your church-lady aunt finds out about your prowess at beer pong or your vacation to Amsterdam, there is also this:

Hear and understand: not what goes into the mouth defiles a man, but what comes out of the mouth, this defiles a man. (Matthew 15:10-11)

And if you'd like to put some frosting on the point, you can always trot out this golden oldie:

He who is without sin among you, let him first cast a stone. (John 8:7)

Note: there is no good reason to tell them what we learned earlier, that Jesus probably never said it. It is in the Bible after all.

And while we are on the topic of morality, you might want to ask Mr. Microphone the following questions about these moral role models from the Old Testament:

1. Why did Abraham pimp out his wife and trick a Pharaoh into sleeping with her in Genesis 12? For that matter, why did Abraham's wife, Sarah, pimp out her maid Hagar to Abraham in Genesis 16?

2. Why did Lot, the biblical poster boy for sexual ethics, offer his two virgin daughters to a crowd of Sodomite sex maniacs in Genesis 19? And why, after their mother was turned into a pillar of salt, did Lot's daughters get him drunk and have incestuous

sex with him in a hillside cave, *on consecutive nights no less,* also in Genesis 19?

3. If onanism (masturbating) is a moral sin, why is it named for Onan, whom God ordered to impregnate his widowed sister-in-law in Genesis 38, then struck dead simply because Onan felt guilty and withdrew from her before finishing and "spilled his seed upon the ground?"

4. Why did King David, the greatest of all Jewish kings, impregnate Bathsheba, a married woman, then arrange for her husband to be killed so he could marry her himself, as described in 2 Samuel 11? While we're at it, why did he dance naked in public before a group of young women in 2 Samuel 6?

***

Before I go, I'd also like to offer this house favorite—a useful generic response to most any muddled mish-mash of Fundamentalist folderol.

You hypocrites! Well did Isaiah prophecy of you, when he said: "This people honors me with their lips, but their hearts are far from me; in vain do they worship me, teaching as doctrines the precepts of men." (Matthew 15:7-9)

Just stop for a second and think about those words straight from the mouth of Jesus: "in vain do they worship me, teaching as doctrines the precepts of men"—in other words, teaching as truth the bullshit of men. *Bravo, Jesus!* You just summed up the most vocal strain of those claiming to follow you. They also say you are coming back. Could you hurry, please? We need more quotes like this one.

And finally, for when you momentarily lack the strength of character to rise above these unjustified curbside assaults and feel the need to dole out some Old Testament vengeance of your own, there is always this horrifying biblical taunt, aimed by the Jews at their historical nemesis, the people of Babylon.

Blessed is he who takes your little ones and dashes them against the rocks! (Psalms 137:9)

Ain't the Old Testament grand?

AFTERWORD

REDEMPTION

And so we draw to a close. You, the outside critic of Christianity who in the past felt vulnerable to Christian proselytizing, are now armed to the teeth and ready to annihilate the next Fundamentalist nitwit foolish enough to mess with you. I won't ask you to consider What Jesus Would Do, but at least keep in mind the rules of war under the Geneva Convention. With great power comes great responsibility.

On the other hand, if you are a well-intentioned Christian you may feel more vulnerable than ever after this no-holds-barred probe of the story of Jesus and the sordid history of Christianity. To be sure, mistakes were made in Jesus's name, but please, step back from the ledge. Allow me to suggest that, as always, you should refer to your Bible. Try starting with Jesus's parable of the departing master who gave money to three servants to safeguard while he was away (Matthew 25:14-30). Two of them risked investing it; they earned profits and their master's favor. The third one, wanting to play it safe, buried the master's money, then dug it up and returned it unchanged, which to the servant's great surprise infuriated the master.

From the beginning this book has targeted you, the timid Christian who, like the fearful servant, perceives risk only in change, forgetting the greater risks of rust and rot when faith is buried under the debris of antiquity. I hope you will feel prodded to dust off and reconsider not just the way you worship and how others perceive you, but also what exactly it is you believe and why you believe it.

A mentally lazy Christian is a poor Christian indeed. Being a Christian carries with it a lifelong responsibility to bring all of one's faculties to bear on the challenges of each new day and the changes of each passing year, guided by Jesus's message of compassion, generosity, humility, and forgiveness. Because if history and this book establish anything, it is that while there is nothing wrong with being a good Christian, there is *everything* wrong with being a lousy one.

And if the thinking Christians who read this book should decide to storm the headquarters of their respective church denominations, demanding an explanation for being deliberately kept in the dark and at times deceived, well, I wouldn't blame them a bit. Plus, it would be great fun for the rest of us to watch.

Finally, we should all remember that in those moments when bleating Fundamentalists are at their absolute worst, they are acting in complete ignorance of the best principles of Christianity. That is to say our ultimate revenge, if you want to jokingly call it that, will always be the knowledge that on a routine daily basis, these people get their own beloved religion, their supposed *raison d'être,* exactly wrong.

Is their behavior redeemable? That's hard to say. At the very least they'd probably need a prolonged dose of their own medicine—shame, repentance, atonement, and *then* undeserved redemption. For how long? Well, two thousand years would be a really good start. Who knows? They might find they like their actual religion. Or they might find they can't live without those beloved features of the Christianity they made up from whole cloth: arrogance, ignorance, snap judgment, greed, materialism, excessive pride, self-pity, public piety, vengefulness, glorification of violence, lust for power, and the one that covers it all: **hypocrisy**.

But should they ever decide to go back to it, we'll be waiting for them, well informed, with our own trusty little book in hand.

ADDITIONAL READING

The New Oxford Annotated Bible.

Anything by Joseph Campbell, e.g. *The Hero with a Thousand Faces, The Masks of God, The Power of Myth.*

Anything by Bart Ehrman, e.g. *Misquoting Jesus: The Story Behind Who Changed the Bible and Why, Jesus Interrupted, Lost Christianities: The Battle for Scripture and the Faiths We Never Knew,* and *Lost Scriptures: Books That Did Not Become the New Testament.*

Elaine Pagels, *Beyond Belief: The Secret Gospel of Thomas.*

Philip Jenkins, *The Lost History of Christianity.*

Reza Aslan, *Zealot.*

Erik Erikson, *Young Man Luther.*

Peter Duffy Eamon, *Saints and Sinners – a History of the Popes.*

William J. Whalen, *Separated Brethren.*

John McManners, *The Oxford Illustrated History of Christianity.*

With special thanks to a little book by Jim Hill and Rand Cheadle, *The Bible Tells Me So.*

KEY TO COVER FIGURES:

1. Joe Guy
2. Referee J.C.
3. Michele Bachmann
4. Pat Robertson
5. Westboro Baptist cretins
6. A cow, somewhere in Iowa
7. Mr. Microphone
8. Ring Gal
9. Where gays get glitter
10. Mr. Mime
11. The illustrator
12. The author
13. John 3:16 sign-waver guy
14. MLK
15. Martin Luther
16. Dr. Freud
17. Prof. Einstein
18. Harvey Milk
19. Matthew Shepard
20. Mary Ellen McCormack
21. Oscar Wilde
22. Karl Marx
23. Rasta Mon
24. The Elusive Q
25. The Warring Trio of First Cousins
26. Sweet Scientist Smokin' Joe
27. The Greatest
28. Mr. Dinosaur
29. Adam
30. Eve
31. Charles Darwin
32. Galileo Galilei
33. Coach Sandusky
34. Lucifer, the morning star
35. Pope Francis
36. Pope Benedict XVI
37. Jerry Falwell
38. James Watt
39. Mr. Lecter
40. Spanish Inquisitor
41. Either a woman who can swim or a witch, doesn't matter
42. Either Moses or Heston, doesn't matter
43. Pointy-headed subhuman
44. Pres. Jefferson
45. Mark Twain
46. A Southern Gentleman
47. His Property